DAY BY DAY
IN THE
Little Way

365 REFLECTIONS ON THE TEACHINGS *of* ST. THÉRÈSE OF LISIEUX

SUSAN BRINKMANN, OCDS

CATHOLIC LIFE INSTITUTE

PRESS
P.O. Box 1173
Pottstown, PA 19464

Copyright © 2020 by Susan Brinkmann

All rights reserved. No part of this publication may be reproduced, distributed or transmitted in any form or by any means, without prior written permission.

Catholic Life Institutes Press
PO Box 1173 Pottstown, PA 19464
www.catholiclifeinstitute.org

Cover Design and Interior Layout by Elizabeth Racine
ElizabethRacine.com

Photo Credit: Cover image of rose by Ina Hoekstra from Pixabay.com

Day by Day in the Little Way/Susan Brinkmann–1st ed.
ISBN-13: 978-1-7336724-7-4

"For simple souls
there must be no
complicated ways."

St. Thérèse of Lisieux

From the Author

Dear Little Soul:

Are you ready for a challenge? How would you like to spend the next year of your life immersed in St. Thérèse of Lisieux's Little Way of Spiritual Childhood?

Day by Day in the Little Way is both a devotional and a practical way to learn the teachings of St. Thérèse. Each day begins with a quote, followed by a short teaching, personal reflection and call-to-action, as well as a prayer to Thérèse. The purpose of this format is to provide you with a miniature formation program. As any spiritual director will tell you, the best formation for the soul is one that includes both the head and the heart, the intelligence and the will. By challenging you to both read and act upon her teachings, you will not only acquire a deeper understanding of spiritual childhood, but you will also gain new insight into your own weaknesses. By praying to Thérèse for the daily grace you need to meet each day's challenge, you will gradually gain the strength to make Thérèse's Little Way your Little Way.

Will you let St. Thérèse form you into one of God's little souls?

It is recommended that you keep a journal during this year to note your progress. What did you learn about the Little Way, and your own littleness, each day? How did you fare when you tried to put that teaching into practice during the day? What did this reveal to you about your own weaknesses? Is this daily challenge helping to make Thérèse's teachings more clear to you? What are you learning that you never knew before? Are you seeing graces from God that you never noticed?

It is my hope that much will be revealed to you during the course of this year, and that each day you will experience your own personal "shower of roses" from the Little Flower of Lisieux.

The Holy Spirit only reveals what we are capable of understanding at the present moment, which is why this book can be used over and over again, each time revealing new insights and inspirations about your journey of faith.

As you begin this journey into the heart and soul of Thérèse, may the Reine des Tout-Petits, the Queen of the Very Little Ones, walk beside you each day and form you into the "flower" God meant for you to be in the garden of His creation.

Susan Brinkmann, OCDS

Sources

Quotations from St. Thérèse of Lisieux found in this book were acquired from the following sources:

St. Thérèse of Lisieux, *Story of a Soul*, translated by John Clarke, OCD (Washington DC: *ICS Publications*, 1972)

Clarke, John OCD, *St. Thérèse of Lisieux: Her Last Conversations* (Washington, DC: *ICS Publications, 1972*)

Quoted by Francois Jamart, OCD, *Complete Spiritual Doctrine of St. Thérèse of Lisieux* (Staten Island, New York: *Alba House*, 1961)

St. Thérèse of Lisieux, *Letters of St. Thérèse of Lisieux*, translated by John Clarke, OCD (Washington DC: *ICS Publications*, 1988)

McClernon, John P., *Sermon in a Sentence* (San Francisco, CA: *Ignatius Press*, 2002)

De Meester, Conrad, With Empty Hands: *The Message of St. Thérèse of Lisieux* (Washington DC: *ICS Publications*, 2002)

Timeline

OF THE

LIFE OF ST. THÉRÈSE OF LISIEUX[1]

1873

January 2 – The birth of Marie-Francoise-Thérèse Martin at 36 Saint Blaise Street, Alencon, France.

January 4 – Thérèse is baptized in the Church of Notre Dame

1877

August 28 – The death of St. Zelie Martin, the mother of Thérèse

November 15 – The Martin family moves to Les Buissonnets (the little bushes), in Lisieux

---

1 St. Thérèse of Lisieux, *Story of a Soul*, translated by John Clarke, OCD (Washington DC: *ICS Publications*, 1972) pgs. 279-288

1880

October 3 – Thérèse enters school at the Benedictine Abbey

1883

March 25 – Easter – Thérèse becomes ill while staying with her cousins

May 13 – Pentecost – Thérèse is cured after seeing a statue of Our Lady smile

1884

May 8 – Thérèse makes her First Holy Communion

June 14 – Thérèse is confirmed by Bishop Hugonin, bishop of Lisieux

1886

December 25 – After midnight Mass, Thérèse receives the grace of conversion that freed her from more than a year of scruples

1887

May 29 (Pentecost) – Thérèse receives permission from her father, St. Louis Martin, to enter Carmel

October 31 – Thérèse visits Bishop Hugonin at Bayeux to request permission to enter Carmel

November 4 – Thérèse travels to Rome with her father and sister, Celine

November 20 – During an audience with Pope Leo XIII, Thérèse asks for permission to enter Carmel at the age of 15

1888

January 1 – Thérèse is granted permission to enter Carmel

April 9 – Thérèse enters the Camel at Lisieux

1889

January 10 – Thérèse receives the habit of Carmel

1890

September 8 – Thérèse makes her profession in Carmel

1894

July 29 – Thérèse's father, St. Louis Martin, dies

1895

During this year, Thérèse begins to write *Story of a Soul*

June 11 – Thérèse makes the offering to Merciful Love

1896

April 2-3 – (Holy Thursday/Good Friday) Thérèse experiences the first hemoptysis in her cell

May 10 – Thérèse dreams of seeing the late foundress of Lisieux, Venerable Anne of Jesus, who tells Thérèse that God is coming to take her home soon.

1897

April – Thérèse falls gravely ill

July 8 – Thérèse is brought to the infirmary

July 30 – Thérèse receives the anointing of the sick

August 19 – Thérèse receives communion for the last time

September 30 – Thérèse dies at 7:20 p.m.

October 4 – Thérèse is buried in the Lisieux cemetery

1898

March 7 – Bishop Hugonin gives permission to publish the Story of a Soul

September 30 – 2,000 copies of *The Story of a Soul* are printed

1899

First favors and cures begin to be reported; pilgrims begin to visit the grave of St. Thérèse to pray

1909

Father Rodrique OCD and Monsignor de Teil are named Postulator and Vice Postulator of the cause of Sister Thérèse

1910

July – Within one year of the opening of Thérèse's cause, the Carmel of Lisieux reports receiving nearly

10,000 letters from around the world regarding favors attributable to Thérèse

September 6 – the remains of St. Thérèse of Lisieux are transferred to a new vault

1914

July – the Carmel of Lisieux is now receiving 200 letters a day about favors attributable to Thérèse

June 10 – Piux X signs the Decree for the Introduction of the Writings of Sister Thérèse

and privately refers to her as "the greatest saint of modern times."

1921

August 14 – Pope Benedict XI declares Sister Thérèse to be Venerable

1923

April 29 – Sister Thérèse of the Child Jesus is beatified by Pope Pius XI who declares her the "star of his pontificate"

1925

May 17 – Thérèse is canonized by Pope Pius XI at St. Peter's in Rome

1927

December 14 – Pope Pius XI proclaims St. Thérèse to be Patroness of all missionaries alongside St. Francis Xavier

1929

Sepember 30 – the cornerstone is laid at the Basilica at Lisieux

1937

July 11 – Papal Legate, Cardinal Pacelli, the future Pope Pius XII, blesses the basilica at Lisieux

1944

May 3 – Pope Pius XII declares St. Thérèse to be the secondary patroness of France alongside St. Joan of Arc

1997

October 14 – Pope John Paul II declares St. Thérèse to be a Doctor of the Church, making her the youngest person to ever receive this distinction.

REFLECTIONS
FOR
January

January 1

"My mission is just beginning, my mission of making others love the good Lord as I love Him and giving to souls my 'Little Way.'"

As I begin this year with Thérèse, I want to take a moment to reflect upon how I can assist in her sacred mission of making God loved in the world. How can I help her? In what way would I love to make her mission my own?

St. Thérèse, give me a new and holy boldness to become your co-worker by embracing your mission of making God loved on earth. Teach me your Little Way so that it may become my Little Way. St. Thérèse, let your mission with me begin!

January 2

*"In the world of souls, the living garden of the Lord,
it pleases Him to create great Saints, who may be
compared with the lilies and the rose;
but He has also created little ones, who
must be content to be daisies or violets."*

❦

Thérèse often used flowers to describe the different kinds of souls and always saw herself as a "little" flower rather than a glorious rose or lily and was always content to be who she was – little. What flower am I in the living garden of the Lord? Am I content to be this flower, or do I think it's due to my own fault that I'm not a rose or a lily?

❦

St. Thérèse, on this your birthday, the best gift I can give you is to ask for your intercession on my behalf, that I might receive the grace to be content with who I am, to accept my limitations without bitterness, and to open my heart to the God who loves me in spite of myself.

❦

Marie-Francois-Thérèse Martin was born on this day in 1873 in the Martin home on 36 Saint Blaise Street in Alencon, France.

January 3

"To be little is not attributing to oneself the virtues that one practices, believing oneself capable of anything, but to recognize that God places this treasure in the hands of His little child to be used when necessary."

The "Little" in the Little Way is all about humility and seeing ourselves for who we really are – not who we wish to be or who we think God expects us to be. We are who we are and everything good in ourselves is a gift from God. Am I willing to accept myself for who I am and let God use me in whatever way He pleases?

St. Thérèse, help me to realize that I can do all things through Him who strengthens me.

January 4

"Everything is a grace."

These four words reveal the secret of the Little Way, the realization that it is only with the help of God's grace that we can become that saints He designed us to be. How fully do I realize this truth? Do I still credit my progress in the spiritual life to my own efforts, or do I realize that everything I have accomplished thus far, including my cooperation with the many graces He has bestowed upon me, is due to Him alone?

St. Thérèse, intercede for me that my eyes may be opened to the truth of who I am so that I might become truly humble of heart.

Thérèse was baptized on this day in 1873 in the church of Notre-Dame. Her sister Marie was her godmother.

January 5

"God is a Father. Allow Him to act as He pleases. He knows well what His very small baby needs."

When I pray, do I permit God to do as He pleases with my requests, or do I tell Him how I want Him to answer me? What does this tell me about my level of trust in God?

St. Thérèse, help me to see God as you did, as your "bon Dieu" and loving Father, so that I can go to Him with my needs and rest assured that He will answer these prayers in the way that is best for me.

January 6

"For having nothing, I shall receive
everything from God."

Do I think I have to "earn" favor from God, or
do I realize that it is exactly my inability to do so
that attracts Him to me? Am I too ashamed of my
weaknesses to ask Him for help?

*St. Thérèse, help me to understand that if I am a person of
good will who sincerely wants to please God, I need not fear the
weaknesses that I am so powerless to overcome because these
sorry parts of me are precisely what attracts God to me.*

January 7

*"The Lord is often pleased to give wisdom
to little ones."*

Sometimes it is the smallest and most innocent heart that is the most capable of absorbing the wisdom of God because in this soul there is found no selfishness or pretense. Why does God usually reveal His mysteries to souls such as these rather than to the learned or those who believe themselves to be more worthy of His favors? Could it be because the little soul is more willing to turn to Him for help? How willing am I to turn to God for the help I need -or do I try too hard to do it myself?

St. Thérèse, you teach us that there is a certain kind of wisdom that only comes from love. Pray for me that my heart may be stripped of all pride so that I may be open to all that God wants to do through me.

January 8

"It is proper to divine love to lower itself; hence, the lower we are, the more we attract God."

❧

None of us like our shortcomings. It is part of the human condition to try to be bigger than we are; but this attitude is antithetical to the Little Way. We need to see – and love – our shortcomings because they attract God's mercy. How do I view my shortcomings? Am I so ashamed of them that I try to hide them from myself and God? Is this because I doubt His mercy, that He wants to heal me of these failings? Do I realize how much it pains Him to see me struggle to "fix" these weaknesses while not asking for the help He so much wants to give?

❧

St. Thérèse, in your Little Way, there is no reason to hide my weaknesses in shame and embarrassment because these dark areas in my soul are what attract God to me. Help me to put my pride aside and to open my woundedness to His healing love.

January 9

"In order to belong to Jesus we must be little, but there are few souls who aspire to remain in that littleness."

❦

It's one thing to be little because that's my lot, but it's quite another to *aspire* to be little. How do I react to my own "littleness" – my inability to do all the great things I think I ought to do in order to become a saint? Instead of accepting who I am, do I impose standards on myself that are too lofty and thus lead me to discouragement? How can I become more realistic in my approach to sanctity?

❦

St. Thérèse, help me to perceive the beauty in authentic littleness, the poverty of spirit that makes a soul fully aware of who it is – and isn't – in the eyes of an infinitely merciful God.

January 10

"No, I'm not a saint. I've never performed the actions of a saint. I am a very little soul upon whom God has bestowed graces; that's what I am."

It seems impossible that Thérèse would think of herself as anything other than a saint, but she did so because she realized that everything good in her came from God. Do I realize that because of this divine truth, God can and will endow me with all the grace I need to achieve sanctity here on earth?

St. Thérèse, you knew from the depth of your being that it was God who made you "the greatest saint of modern times." Pray that I might not squander the graces God is sending me to make me a saint.

On this day in 1889, Thérèse received the habit of Carmel.

January 11

"It is to recognize our nothingness, to expect everything from God as a little child expects everything from its father; it is to be disquieted about nothing..."

It never even occurs to a child to doubt that his parent will take care of his every need. This is not due to pretention on the child's part, but is due to the innate and unquestioning trust that he has in his parents. Do I have that kind of confidence in God?

Little Flower, intercede for me before God the Father and ask Him to help me to see Him as merciful father in whom I can turn for all of my needs.

January 12

"It is only when His children ignore their constant lapses and make a habit of them and fail to ask His pardon that Christ grieves over them."

❦

Accepting our weaknesses doesn't mean that we can become complacent in our spiritual life. The Little Way is founded on the premise of good will, meaning that the soul is always striving to please God, but falls short because of its weaknesses. Am I a person of good will? Do I sincerely repent of my sins and shortcomings, ask God for help, and make firm resolutions to cooperate with His grace?

❦

St. Thérèse, I'm so little and fall often. Pray for me that I may never tire of trying to please God or take His love and mercy for granted.

January 13

"O Lord, You would not inspire me with a desire which could not be realized; therefore, in spite of my littleness, I can aim at being a saint."

We are made in the image and likeness of God and are therefore designed to achieve whatever level of sanctity God has willed for us. How much do I desire to fulfill God's dream for my sanctity? Do I want to become a saint? Does this aspiration make me feel uncomfortable, unworthy, or conflicted inside? How important is it to me to achieve the sanctity God willed for me?

St. Thérèse, you wanted to become a saint, even while knowing that it was impossible for you without God's help. Intercede for me before God and ask Him to give me the grace to both desire sainthood, and to be confident that He can and will make this possible for me.

January 14

*"The strong God loves to show His power
by making use of nothing."*

❧

Scripture is replete with stories of how the Almighty uses the weak to show His power, from the stammering Moses to the insecure Gideon and little shepherd boy known as David. How willing am I to let God use my weakness to show His power, or am I too busy trying to cover up my shortcomings so no one will see them?

❧

St. Thérèse, instead of hiding your weaknesses, you not only loved and embraced them, but you willingly let the world see them just to prove how much God can do in little souls that are fully surrendered to His will. Intercede for me that I might receive this grace from God and cooperate with it in order to let Him use me to show His power to our broken world.

January 15

"My mortification consisted in checking my self-will; keeping back an impatient word, doing little things for those around me without knowing, and countless things like that."

Notice how St. Thérèse chose seemingly little and inconspicuous ways to mortify her self-love by stifling her impatience and making hidden acts of kindness for which she would receive no credit. How can I imitate her today?

St. Thérèse, help me to take notice of all the opportunities that arise in the course of my day to put your little way of mortification into practice. Help me to make this practice into a "holy habit."

January 16

"It is my weakness that gives me confidence."

The Little Way teaches us see weakness in a whole new light. Instead of letting our shortcomings fill us with shame and embarrassment, they should give us hope in the mercy of our God who longs to help us do what we cannot accomplish on our own. The only thing we need to do is ask Him for help. This truth should be a cause for joy, not sorrow! Does this thought fill me with a new sense of confidence and hope?

Dearest Thérèse, help me to avoid dwelling on my weaknesses so that I may focus more on the mercy of God. Pray that I might be so convinced of His mercy that I no longer shrink in shame, but run with confidence into the loving arms of my Heavenly Father.

January 17

"The remembrance of my weakness is so constantly present to me that there is no room for vanity."

❧

Thérèse never dwelled on her weaknesses, but she never forgot them either. Do I keep my weaknesses in mind so that I might remain grounded in the truth about who I am in the eyes of God? Or am I uncomfortable with my weaknesses and prefer to dwell on my good points instead? Could giving in to these feelings become a temptation to vanity?

❧

St. Thérèse, help me to remain mindful of how weak I am while not becoming morbid and pessimistic about myself. You loved yourself – both your strengths and weaknesses. Pray for me that I may learn how to do the same.

January 18

"When we calmly accept the humiliation of being imperfect, Your grace, O Lord, returns at once."

In the spiritual realm, relying on ourselves rather than on God's help to achieve perfection is a fool's folly and serves only to block the grace we so desperately need. Am I standing in the Lord's way in my faith life? Do I turn to Him for help as often as I should? Am I trying to perfect myself on my own?

Little Flower, show me if I am standing in God's way by trying to achieve sanctity on my own. Pray that I might learn to turn to Jesus for all of my spiritual needs.

January 19

"I am glad to feel so imperfect and to need your mercy so much!"

❧

Is my pride standing in the way of facing my imperfections? Am I blaming myself for not being better, which is just another manifestation of pride and self-love. Am I willing to just accept the fact that I can't "fix it" without God's help? Could this be because I secretly doubt His mercy?

❧

St. Thérèse, even though my imperfections are due to my own weakness, the powerlessness I feel in overcoming them is precisely what endears me to God. Like a parent who wants to help their little one to walk, He longs for me to say, "I can't do it! Help me!" Pray that I may put aside all fear and doubt in His mercy and run to Him for the help I need.

January 20

"What pleases Jesus is to see me love my littleness and poverty, the blind hope that I have in His mercy. This is my only treasure."

Do I love my littleness and poverty? Am I able to embrace those aspects of myself with the same blind hope that Thérèse had? Might this be a special grace to ask for today?

St. Thérèse, please intercede for me before God that I might receive the grace to hope in Him without reservation, with all of my heart and soul, not just in spite of my littleness, but because of it!

January 21

"The only thing for which you will not be envied is the lowest place; therefore, the lowest place is the only one where there is no vanity and affliction of spirit."

❦

Everyone loves recognition, particularly when we think we deserve it, but being noticed is not always the best outcome in the spiritual realm because it exposes us to the temptation to exalt ourselves. Do I seek out the lowest place, or do I like to be noticed and favored? Do I get upset when people seem to overlook me, or do I use these and other similar slights to mortify my pride?

❦

St. Thérèse, you were content to be assigned the lowest duties in the convent, to sweep up the cobwebs even though you were terrified of spiders. Help me to overcome my fear of being overlooked or denied the praise I think I deserve and calmly accept only the praise God permits me to receive.

January 22

*"I beg you, divine Jesus, send me a humiliation
every time I try to put myself above others."*

How often do I elevate myself at the expense of
others? Do my insecurities make me prone to
exalting myself more than I deserve? Do I have the
courage to mortify this habit by making Thérèse's
prayer my own?

*St. Thérèse, pray for me that I may overcome my penchant for
esteem in the eyes of man so that I might concentrate on gaining the
only esteem that really matters, that of the God Who created me.*

January 23

*"I expect as much from God's justice
as from His mercy."*

Thérèse understood God's justice to mean His fairness in taking into account a person's intentions, circumstances, etc., rather than His severity in punishment. How I do I perceive God's justice? Do I expect as much from His justice as from His mercy?

Dear Thérèse, I need your intercession to ask God for the grace to understand the beauty of His justice, that it is not something I need to fear, but something for which I should praise Him. Help me to expect as much from His justice as I do from His mercy!

January 24

"When we commit a fault we must not attribute it to a physical cause, such as illness or the weather, but we must attribute it to our own lack of perfection."

Do I make excuses for my faults and failures? Do I face my limitations squarely or do I make excuses for myself and blame others or certain circumstances for my failings?

Dear Thérèse, help me to understand my failings as being a part of my human condition so that when I fall, I might run to God and His healing mercy rather than hide behind a long list of clever rationalizations.

January 25

*"A lack of confidence offends Jesus
and wounds His heart."*

Am I confident in God's love for me, or do I think it's conditioned upon my "performance?" Do I have faith in His Word and trust Him enough to abandon myself, my possessions, my loved ones, to His care? If not, what might be holding me back?

Dear Thérèse, you placed all your hope in God and His mercy. Plead for me before God that I will make good use of the faith He gifted to me at the moment of my Baptism. Help me to spend quality time with Him in prayer so that my trust and confidence in Him will grow and strengthen.

January 26

"We never have too much confidence in the good Lord who is so powerful and merciful. We obtain from Him as much as we hope for."

What do I hope for from God? Do I hope for it all, believing that He is capable of doing great things in me, or do I short-change him by asking only for what I think I deserve?

St. Thérèse, teach me to hope for everything from our good God, knowing that He can provide me with all the graces I need to achieve great things for Him even in spite of myself.

January 27

"He measures His gifts according to the amount of confidence He finds in us."

What spiritual gifts do I yearn to receive from God? The grace of a stronger faith, a deeper trust, a more profound peace? Do my feelings of unworthiness erode my confidence in Him and make me feel as if I'm asking for too much?

Dearest Thérèse, you had such great confidence in God, it's no wonder that He filled you with so much grace! Pray for me that I might let go of any tendencies within myself to try to "earn" God's favors and focus instead on how much He wants to help me achieve sanctity.

January 28

"I shall always sing, even should my flowers be gathered from the midst of thorns."

It's not always easy to accept the ups and downs of life with a smile, but Thérèse strove to do so as often as she could out of love for God and neighbor. How can I imitate her today?

Little Flower, you mortified your self-love in so many little ways, and always out of love for God and neighbor. Open my eyes to the many opportunities that arise in the course of my day to do the same — and to do so with great love for God, my neighbor — and you!

January 29

"To humble ourselves, to suffer our imperfections with patience, that is true sanctity, the source of peace."

❧

Unlike the Little Way which teaches us how to be at peace with our weaknesses, the failure to accept ourselves and our imperfections can be a source of great inner anxiety and uneasiness. How can I be more gentle and patient with myself today?

❧

St. Thérèse, you were never harsh with yourself for being little. Instead, you cherished this about yourself because it made you instinctively turn to God and pray for His mercy. Intercede for me that I may learn this "holy habit" from you!

January 30

"Jesus bears...[our imperfections] patiently; He does not like teaching us everything at once, but normally enlightens us a little at a time."

❦

Am I comparing myself to standards that are much too high for me? Do I get frustrated with myself for not being more advanced spiritually? In what ways might I be "pushing against grace" and not letting the Lord lead me in the way and time of His choosing?

❦

Dear Thérèse, you were content to be Jesus' little flower and didn't strive after a holiness that was unsuitable for you. Teach me to be content with who I am in the "garden" of God and spend my time learning how to bloom where I have been planted.

January 31

"I am very poor. It is the good Lord who provides for me from moment to moment with the amount of help I need to practice virtue."

❧

Thérèse was a big advocate of living in the present moment because she knew that this is where God dwells, and where God dwells, there we find all the grace we need for each moment of our day. How much time during the day is spent in the present moment, savoring the presence of God within me? Am I always rushing ahead, or dwelling on the past? Do I realize that God has provided everything I need for every moment of every day?

❧

St. Thérèse, pray for me that I might learn how to be more aware of the presence of God within me during the day so that I can realize His Providence in "real time."

REFLECTIONS
FOR
February

February 1

"If a little flower could speak, it seems to me that it would tell us quite simply all that God has done for it, without hiding any of its gifts. It would not, under the pretext of humility, say that it was not pretty, or that it had not a sweet scent, that the sun had withered its petals, or the storm bruised its stem, if it knew that such were not the case."

In the Little Way, everything is relative. If the smallest flower is the best smallest flower it can be, it is just as good as the beautiful rose that is the best rose it could be. Do I understand this parity and realize that I can be just as magnificent as the rose if I'm the best pansy or violet that I can be? Does this help me to accept myself more, and to appreciate the gifts God has given me rather than seeing only my deficiencies and putting myself down?

St. Thérèse, help me to accept who I am and to spend time today praising God for the beauty of my littleness.

February 2

"Trust and trust alone should lead us to love"

Thérèse saw God as a compassionate and merciful Father whom she could turn to for help no matter what problems she was facing in life, and it was out of this trusting relationship that her love for Him grew. Who is the first person I turn to when I'm in trouble and in need? Is it God, or is He further down the list?

Dear Thérèse, pray for me that I might learn how to turn to God first when I'm in need, and then give Him the praise He deserves for the people He sends to help me.

February 3

"O Jesus…How could there be any limit to my trust?"

It's impossible not to trust a God as benevolent as ours. When was the last time you counted your blessings? When you add them all up and see just how much God has done for you, how does this impact your willingness to trust Him in the future?

St. Thérèse, you never doubted that God would take care of you, one way or the other. After all of the confirmation He has given me, help me to give Him the trust He deserves.

February 4

*"How necessary it is for a person to be
detached from and elevated above herself
in order not to experience any harm."*

Our culture glorifies individualism and inspires a self-centered lifestyle that is the antithesis of the Great Commandment of Jesus to love God and neighbor. How can I forget myself today in order to be more focused on the needs of others and how God may want me to respond to those needs?

St. Thérèse, there's no selfishness in your Little Way. It's all about loving God and others. Help me to control my self-love and tendency to focus on myself today so that my eyes may be more open and alert to the needs of others.

February 5

"It is impossible for me to become great, so I must bear with myself and my many imperfections."

❦

Ironically, Thérèse did become great, not for overcoming her imperfections, but for learning how to accept them and leaving us her Little Way to help us imitate her example. How can I make an extra effort today to bear with myself and my many imperfections?

❦

St. Thérèse, pray for me that I might spend my time learning to bear with myself rather than worrying about how great I think I'm supposed to be?

February 6

"I will try to find a lift by which I may be raised unto God, for I am too small to climb the steep stairway of perfection."

Do I see God and His grace as my only hope for sainthood, or am I still trying to do it myself? Am I afraid to admit that the stairway to perfection is just too steep for me? Do I think I might be penalized in some way for not being able to make the climb?

Little Flower, you never tired of asking God for help, an attitude which could only come from a sincere acceptance of your limitations. Pray for me that I might experience this level of acceptance so that I will never hesitate to ask God for what I need.

February 7

"To reach heaven I need not become great; on the contrary, I must remain little, I must become even smaller than I am."

❦

In this quote, Thérèse is not teaching us to become even more imperfect; rather, she is teaching us how to become ever more aware of our littleness, thus deepening our humility. How aware am I of my weaknesses? Does fear of reprisal or shame keep me from looking squarely at my weaknesses? What does this tell me about the level of my confidence in God?

❦

Thérèse, you knew that the only way to heaven was by relying on the mercy of God, a belief that was founded in your calm acceptance of just how much you needed Him. Pray for me that I, too, might not be afraid to see myself as I really am, and to put all my trust in God's mercy.

February 8

"You see what I am capable of, O my God, and so You will be obliged to carry me in Your arms."

Confidence is the hallmark of the Little Way! Thérèse firmly believed that when God saw one of His children floundering in their weakness, He would react just like any good parent and rush to their aid. Do I have this confidence? Do I trust that God wants to help me in my weakness, or do I perceive Him as being disappointed or angry with me because I can't do any better?

St. Thérèse, intercede for me that God will grant me the grace of a deep and abiding confidence in His paternal love for me.

February 9

"What difference does it make, O Lord, if I fall at every instant? It will make me realize my weakness and I shall derive great profit from it."

❦

Thérèse was doted upon by her family while growing up and admitted that she was quite spoiled – and sometimes acted that way! Whenever she acted poorly, she quickly apologized, repented, then got back on her feet and used the occasion to remind herself just how much she needed God's help. How do I react when I fall? Do I chastise myself for hours on end, or do I admit my mistake, repent, then get up and start anew?

❦

Dearest Thérèse, help me to fall like you, humbly and intelligently. Instead of wasting time getting mad at myself, teach me to spend that time seeing myself for who I truly am, and then thanking God for having spared me a worse fall.

February 10

"Yes, all must be kept for You with jealous care, because it is so sweet to work for You alone!

Thérèse was so focused on God that her every move, even her love for others, was done for His sake. This is the essence of simplicity, which is so much a part of the Little Way. It is a gradual stripping of all attachment to self and others until we become wholly focused on loving God, living for Him and pleasing Him in all things. Where am I at in this process? What are the intentions behind the work that I do and the leisure that I enjoy? Do I see all as a gift from God for which He ought to be thanked and praised? What can I do today to become more focused on pleasing God?

Dear Thérèse, my whole life revolves around me. I sometimes forget that everything I have was given to me by God. Help me to see all as His gift, and to enjoy these gifts with jealous care, because they belong to Him Whom I was put on earth to love and to serve.

February 11

"O Jesus, obedience is the compass You have given me to direct me safely to the eternal shore."

❦

Obedience has nothing to do with being a door-mat or behaving like a lemming. Obedience is all about humbling oneself to the will of God as it is revealed to us in all of the circumstances of our lives. How well do I obey my lawful superiors, civilian authorities, the teachings of the Church? Do I only obey someone when I agree with them or when I think they deserve to have authority over me?

❦

St. Thérèse, your saintly eyes perceived the hand of God in all those who had authority over you in life — from your father and older siblings, to your school teachers, pastors, and your superiors in Carmel. You even obeyed the Church authorities when they refused to admit you to Carmel at the age of 15! Help me to behave as humbly as you did, even when I disagree, and to never forget that it is God who placed this person in authority over me.

February 12

"What a joy it is for me to fix my glance upon You and then to accomplish Your will."

❦

For Thérèse, the easiest way to accept God's will, even when it meant that she would die at a young age from tuberculosis of both the lungs and the intestines, was to never forget that His every decision for her life was rooted in His eternal love for her. When the unexpected happens in my life, how do I respond? While it's perfectly human to get upset at first, do I pray through those feelings and refocus my attention on the fact that a "all things work for good for those who love God?" (Romans 8:28)

❦

St. Thérèse, pray for me that I might fix my eyes upon the Lord at all times, especially during dark times when I can't see Him or feel Him. Pray that God will strengthen my faith so that I will trust in His love for me even when I feel betrayed and afraid.

February 13

"I always feel...the same bold confidence of becoming a great saint because I don't count on my merits, since I have none, but I trust in Him who is Virtue and Holiness."

Thérèse put no limits on how much she asked of God, not because she thought she deserved it, but because she knew this is how much God wishes to give us. To ask for sainthood was no exception. Have you ever asked God to make you a saint? Could this be the day you do so?

Dear Thérèse, give me a sip of your holy boldness so that I can ask God to grant me all the blessings He wishes to give me, not the blessings I think I deserve.

February 14

"To be His, one must remain little, little like a drop of dew! Oh! How few are the souls who aspire to remain little in this way!"

Little children are naturally humble, trusting, and abandoned to their parents – all qualities that are inherent in the Little Way. How difficult it is for us to aspire to littleness in a world that exalts status and prominence. Am I able to understand how being little in the eyes of the world is to be great in the eyes of God?

Dear Thérèse, help me to care more about how God sees me than how the world perceives me!

February 15

"If I'm not loved, that's just too bad! I tell the whole truth, and if anyone doesn't wish to know the truth, let her not coming looking for me."

There was not a duplicitous bone in Thérèse's body. She was always sincere and honest with others, even when it was difficult to do so. Am I honest and upfront with others, even when it means being politically incorrect? Do I hide the Truth when it's too inconvenient to tell? Do I ever behave in a two-faced manner, pretending to be someone I'm not, just to save face?

Dear Thérèse, in this day and age, Christian morality is something that is derided and mocked. I find it so hard to speak up for Christ when I risk losing the respect of others. Please ask the Holy Spirit to strengthen in me the gift of courage so that I might speak the truth in love no matter what it costs me.

February 16

"We should never allow a kindness to degenerate into weakness."

Thérèse would never excuse wrongdoing just to be "kind" to someone and spare their feelings. True love for our neighbor puts their eternal life above momentary feelings. How do I respond to situations where practicing my faith may bring ridicule or rebuke? Do I stand firm or do I have a tendency to "go along to get along?"

St. Thérèse, I'm just too weak to take a stand when I ought to do so. Even though I love Jesus, I still love myself and my reputation too much. Intercede for me that I might receive the grace to put myself aside so that I can love Jesus with my whole heart.

February 17

"[When] we can say, without any boasting, that we have received very special graces and lights; we stand in the truth and see things in the proper light."

❦

Thérèse never took credit for her Little Way but gave all the glory to God. Do I see my spiritual progress as being the result of graces and insight from God, or do I credit myself for my prayer and fasting habits, for all the books, conferences and courses in which I've partaken?

❦

St. Thérèse, ask God to grant me the ability to stand in the truth and to see everything about me and my spiritual progress in the proper light, that all is a gift from God, including my cooperation with all the graces He's given me.

February 18

"I do everything for God, and in this way
I can lose nothing…"

Thérèse realized the futility of trying to satisfy oneself because the human condition leaves us forever unsatisfied. Instead, she made her every work, prayer, and moment of leisure into an act of love for God. In this way, she made reparation for the sad indifference of so many Christians and brought comfort to the Sacred Heart of Jesus. What can I do for love of God today?

Dear Thérèse, your love for God inspires me to imitate your selflessness in all that I do today. Intercede for me that I might cooperate with all the grace God is sending me so that I too can say, "I have lost nothing because I have given everything to Him."

February 19

"I love Him so much that I'd like to please Him without His being aware of it. When He knows it and sees it, He is obliged to reward me, and I don't want Him to have to go to this trouble."

Only the Little Flower of Jesus could have conceived of such a tender sentiment as this! She wanted so much to please God – just for His sake and not for a reward – that she wished she could do so without Him knowing it! How much can you do for God today just for love of Him, rather than for a reward?

St. Thérèse, I want to love God the way you did, deeply and authentically. Pray for me that my relationship with God will blossom into one of genuine love.

February 20

"To the right and to the left, I throw to my little birds the good grain that God places in my hands. And then I let things take their course."

Thérèse was the mistress of formation in Lisieux and is referring here to the novices she was directing, but her advice applies even more to those of us who are in the world. When I evangelize, do I try to control the outcome, or do I trust God enough to let Him decide if my efforts will end in failure or success? Do I understand that God's ways are not my ways and that He knows what is best for the souls who cross my path? Do I do my part and then stand back and let God do His?

Dear Thérèse, I want to help God to save souls, but I too often get in His way by trying to control how the person will respond to my efforts. Please pray for me that I learn how to put my expectations aside and let Him take charge of the souls He loves so much more than I ever could.

February 21

"O Lord, when I feel nothing, when I am incapable of praying or practicing virtue, then is the moment to look for small occasions, nothings, to give You pleasure."

❧

Thérèse knew how easy it is to pray when one feels close to God, but when those consolations evaporate and our hearts turn hard and dry, this is when our love and faithfulness is put to the test. How do I respond to God on days when I can't "feel" His closeness, when I find little pleasure in the practice of virtue? Do I become sullen and sad, or do I make an effort to show my love for Him in whatever way I can?

❧

Dear Thérèse, your prayer life in the convent was dry and difficult, and yet it was here that you developed the Little Way and acquired sainthood. Help me to understand that learning how to love God for His sake means remaining faithful even when I must do so without any sensual satisfaction.

February 22

"Oh how little God is loved on this earth, even by priests and religious! No, God isn't loved very much."

Thérèse wanted so much to see God loved in the world that she promised to "spend her heaven doing good on earth" in order to "make Love loved." Does it sadden me to notice how little God is loved in the world? Do I try to make up for this neglect through acts of reparation? Do I pray daily for the conversion of hearts? What more can I do today to "make Love loved"?

Dear Thérèse, I want to make your mission my own and do whatever I can to make God loved in the world. Show me how I can help you. Open my eyes to all the opportunities that will arise today to offer God my loving thanks for the blessings He has bestowed upon our cold-hearted world.

February 23

"Lord, help me simplify my life by learning what you want me to be and then becoming that person."

In our day and age, we complicate our lives with a variety of gimmicks that promise to unlock the secrets of our personality or our future, but Thérèse knew better. She went straight to the Source for this information and implored the God who owned the blueprint of her life to show her who she was meant to be and how she might become that person. Have I ever asked God to do the same for me? Can this be the moment to do so?

Dear Thérèse, you knew that the only way to truly find yourself was to do so in the God who created you. Help me to search in the right places for a deeper understanding of who I am and why I'm here by invoking God whose plan for me "is for your welfare, not for woe" (Jeremiah 29:11).

February 24

"To love is to give everything. It's to give our self."

Thérèse understood that in order to love as Jesus loved, we must get beyond "warm fuzzy" feelings. Authentic love is an act of the will, a decision to give all without counting the cost. Is there someone special in my life to whom I "give all?" Have I ever considered loving God in this way?

St. Thérèse, intercede for me and ask God to give me the grace to put my needs aside so that I can love Him, and my neighbor, more perfectly.

February 25

"I'm very certain that Our Lord didn't say any more to His Apostles through His instructions and His physical presence than He says to us through His good inspirations and His grace."

❦

Thérèse never had a spiritual director. Instead, she found all of the instruction and inspiration she needed by reading Scripture. In fact, several verses in Scripture played a critical role in the formation of the Little Way of Spiritual Childhood. How much time do I spend reflecting on the word of God? Is reading Scripture a regular part of my daily prayer life? If I made more time for it, might it help me to understand Jesus – and His will for me – a little better?

❦

St. Thérèse, the Lord revealed the Little Way to you through several key passages of Scripture. Help me to make the time to read His Word so that I might receive the guidance I need to make the right choices in both my spiritual and material life.

February 26

*"Before dying by the sword, let us die by
means of pin-pricks."*

❧

The Cross of Christ does not necessarily mean
dramatic and bloody suffering; rather, it usually
means those little daily irritations, frustrations,
and disappointments we all experience. How do
I respond to my daily crosses? Do I dismiss them
because they seem so little, or do I recognize them
as valuable sufferings to be endured for love of God
and for my own growth in the spiritual life? How
can I put my little daily crosses to good use today?

❧

*Dear Thérèse, you tried never to miss an opportunity to
suffer for God. Even though I often cringe at the thought of
suffering, pray for me that I might humbly accept what I am
able to suffer, rather than torment myself over what I think I
should suffer!*

February 27

*"I don't see my beauty at all; I see only the graces
I've received from God."*

Thérèse was said to have been a very attractive woman; however, the only beauty she concerned herself with was that of the soul. How much time do I spend focused on my physical appearance? Could some of that time be better spent asking God for the graces I need to beautify my soul?

Little Flower, the eyes of your heart were always turned toward God, and this made you able to see Him everywhere – in everything and everyone, including yourself. Ask God to give me the grace to open the eyes of my heart so that I, too, may recognize all the graces He has given me.

February 28

"God gives me courage in proportion to my sufferings. I feel at this moment I couldn't suffer any more, but I'm not afraid, since if they increase, He will increase my courage at the same time."

Even during the worst days of her physical sufferings, when the tuberculosis had ravaged her lungs and intestines and made even breathing a painful ordeal, Thérèse never stopped believing that God would help her, in whatever way He chose. Am I this confident when things are going wrong? How much do I believe that God wants to help me, or am I too convinced that I must first earn it, or achieve a certain standard before He will do so. Do I know He wants to help me *now, this very minute*, whether I think I deserve it or not?

St. Thérèse, pray for me that I might acquire your great confidence in God! Ask God to reveal to me what is preventing me from truly opening up my heart and trusting Him the way He deserves.

February 29 (leap year)

"I love everything that God gives me."

⬥

This simple statement is not nearly as easy to live as it is to read! Do I really love everything God gives me, including the unexpected disappointments, the daily frustrations, the broken dreams, and painful losses? Do I need to take this to prayer today?

⬥

St. Thérèse, some things have happened to me in my life that make it very difficult for me to forget, and I often wonder why God allowed it. Please pray for me that I might receive the grace to realize that, just as He promises in Scripture, something good can, and will, come out of those dark moments.

REFLECTIONS
FOR
March

March 1

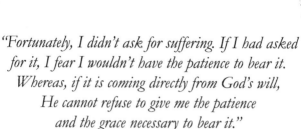

*"Fortunately, I didn't ask for suffering. If I had asked
for it, I fear I wouldn't have the patience to bear it.
Whereas, if it is coming directly from God's will,
He cannot refuse to give me the patience
and the grace necessary to bear it."*

In spite of her tender age, Thérèse had a spiritual
maturity beyond her years and understood that
asking for suffering is often a manifestation of pride.
Instead, we should wait for the Crosses Jesus has
prepared for us, which always come with enough
grace to bear them. How prudent am I about the
penances I take upon myself? Do I discuss this first
with my spiritual director or a close spiritual friend?
Might I be trying to impress God (and myself)
instead of taking on a penance to atone for my sins?

*St. Thérèse, even though you lived during a time when harsh
penances were the norm in the Church, you never hid the fact
that you were unable to perform these practices. Even wearing
a tiny studded cross for a day left you feeling ill. Help me to
discern God's will for me during this penitential season, and to
never lose sight of why I'm performing my penance – to repent
of my sins and console the Heart of Jesus.*

March 2

"I prefer to practice mortification in a manner that leaves my mind more free for God."

When we give up too much food or leisure, it can disturb our equilibrium and make us so preoccupied with the suffering that our minds are no longer free for communion with God. Are my penances disturbing my peace and interrupting my prayer life? Might I have taken on too much? Do I need to humble myself and make a few adjustments to my Lenten practices?

St. Thérèse, there's only one right way to suffer for Christ – in peace. Help me to find my peace and not be ashamed if I can't take on as much penance as I would like. Pray for me that I might be content to be "little" and to offer my "nothings" with as much love as I am capable.

March 3

"O Lord, You do not like to make us suffer, but You know it is the only way to prepare us to know You as You know Yourself, to prepare us to become like You."

To carry the cross of Christ means to learn how to die to self – and whatever suffering this total self-offering might entail - in order to live for God and neighbor. As Thérèse says, it's the only way to know Jesus as He knows Himself. What act of self-giving love can I make today that will make someone's day brighter – and make me more like Jesus?

Dear Thérèse, you understood that in order to truly love as Jesus loved, it meant dying to yourself, to your desires and vanities. If there was an easier way, Jesus would surely show us. Help me to follow Him even though His path is sometimes difficult and not the road I would have chosen.

March 4

"*Each new suffering, each pang of the heart, is a gentle wind to bear to You, O Jesus, the perfume of a soul that loves You.*"

Even the smallest sacrifice, done for love, is enormous in Jesus' eyes. Instead of looking for big things to suffer today, what little inconveniences can I offer Jesus for no other reason than because I love Him?

St. Thérèse, even though you were a little soul, you had the valiant heart of an eagle — and it was filled with love for God. Please ask Jesus to forgive me for the self-love that still crowds Him out of my heart and to grant me the grace of true love for God.

March 5

"What a favor, my Jesus, and how You must love me to send me suffering!"

❦

Do I see suffering as a gift from God, or do I see it as an annoyance and something to avoid? Can I devote this day to accepting all of the annoying little inconveniences, aches and pains, and unexpected disappointments without complaint?

❦

St. Thérèse, your eyes were so fixed on the mercy of God that you were unable to see Him except through this lens. Help me to understand that even when I'm suffering as a result of my own sin, this too is a gift from God because it enables me to truly repent and make amends for having hurt Him.

March 6

*"I am happy not to be free from suffering here;
suffering united with love is the only thing that seems
desirable to me in this vale of tears."*

❦

Thérèse did nothing to avoid suffering and calmly
accepted whatever misery came her way in the
course of a day. Does suffering make me glum and
sad? How can I bear today's crosses more cheerfully?

❦

*St. Thérèse, pray for me that I may have the patience to bear
whatever suffering might come my way today so that I will
accept it calmly and lovingly.*

March 7

"Far from complaining to You of the crosses you send me, I cannot fathom the infinite love which has moved you to treat me so."

When suffering came to Thérèse, her first reaction was probably just as human as ours – to recoil from it – but she quickly recovered herself and looked beyond the pain to see the loving hand of God. Do I see God's infinite love for me in the sufferings of my life?

Dearest Thérèse, my eyes are blinded by pain and I'm unable to see anything through the misery of the moment. Pray for me that I might receive the grace of a new vision that enables me to see God's hand in every suffering and know that if I accept the lot I have been dealt, God will make it all work for my good.

March 8

"O Lord, do not let me waste the trial You send me; it is a gold mine I must exploit."

No matter what kind of trial she was undergoing, Thérèse always looked for a way to make something good come of it. What good can I find in the trials I will face on this day?

St. Thérèse, for such a little soul, you were so heroic in suffering! Could it have been because you knew better than to rely on yourself and looked to God for the grace you needed to turn every trial into a victory? Pray for me that I might learn to do the same!

March 9

"On the way to Calvary, You fell three times; and I, a poor little child, do I not wish to be like you? Should I not wish to fall a hundred times to prove to You my love, rising up again with more strength than before my fall?"

In Thérèse's eyes, to fall is normal for a child. In fact, this is often how a child learns. Thérèse knew that for adults, the secret is to fall like a child, to make every fall count by learning as much as possible from it, and then getting right back on our feet again. When I fall, do I feel sorry for myself, or do I learn from my mistakes, resolve to do better with God's help, then get back up and try again?

Dear Thérèse, pray for me that God will grant me the perseverance and patience I need to put up with myself and my many weaknesses and to never give way to discouragement.

March 10

"I want to abase myself humbly and submit my will to others, not contradicting them nor asking if they have the right to give me orders. No one had this right over You and yet You were obedient, not only to the Blessed Virgin and St. Joseph, but even to Your executioners."

Thérèse understood that the virtue of obedience is never belittling. When we obey those God has put in charge of us, regardless of whether we agree with them or like them, it empowers us because by doing so, we fully embrace the will of God even when it costs us our life as it did Jesus Christ. How do I respond to those who are in lawful authority over me? Do I realize that I am obligated to obey in all instances except sin?

St. Thérèse, sometimes it's very hard for me to obey my superiors, especially when I don't think they deserve their authority. Help me to see through these veils of deception and see God's loving hand in those He gives authority over me.

March 11

"[When] we observe in ourselves a desire for something brilliant, let us humbly take our place with the imperfect and know that we are weak souls who must be sustained every instant by God."

❧

Human nature loves to be esteemed and looked up to by others, but we must never lose sight of the fact that our accomplishments are due to our cooperation with God's grace, not our own efforts. How much do I like to take credit for my accomplishments? Do I forget that my talents are gifts from God to be used for His glory and not my own?

❧

St. Thérèse, even though you did great things, you lived a humble and hidden life that was devoted to doing God's will. Pray for me that I might always remember Who made my success possible for me.

March 12

"...[H]ow sweet and merciful the Lord really is, for He did not send me this trial until the moment I was capable of bearing it."

Thérèse knew that there was no point in worrying in advance about what she had to suffer. Instead, she believed God's promise that He would "not let you be tried beyond your strength" (1 Cor 10:13). When I am undergoing trial, am I tempted to give in to fear and anxious forethought about how things might turn out? Do I need to ask God to give me the grace to trust Him more?

Dear Thérèse, even at the end of your life, when you were suffering terribly from disease, you trusted that Jesus would never lay a cross upon your shoulders without giving you the strength to carry it. When I am under trial, help me to remember this promise and pray that I might have the grace to truly believe it.

March 13

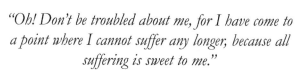

"Oh! Don't be troubled about me, for I have come to a point where I cannot suffer any longer, because all suffering is sweet to me."

❧

No one loves to suffer, except for those whose love for another is so great, such as a mother for a child, that they would gladly endure anything for the sake of their beloved, a sentiment that makes suffering seem "sweet." Is there someone in my life for whom I feel this kind of deep love? Does this help me to realize how suffering can be sweet rather than bitter?

❧

Little Flower, you loved Jesus so much that it was a joy to offer Him the sufferings of your day. Instead of focusing on my pain or discomfort or inconvenience, help me to focus on Him and the tender love that He has shown for me so that I will bear these crosses patiently and lovingly.

March 14

*"Even though you should fall one hundred times,
to prove your love for Him, rise each time
with even greater strength."*

Thérèse knew that God often allows us to fall because we need to be reminded about how weak we are, and how much we need His help. When understood in this light, it's much easier to get back on our feet, knowing that each time we do, we get a little stronger. How do I respond to myself when I fall? Am I too hard on myself? How quickly do I get back up? Do I realize how much spiritual strength I can acquire by falling humbly and patiently?

Dear Thérèse, even though you acknowledged and even loved your weaknesses because of the mercy it drew from God, you never let those weaknesses dampen your indomitable spirit. Help me to resist the temptation to become discouraged over my faults and to use these lapses in such a way that I will have gained more from falling than if I had never fallen at all!

March 15

"It's only through prayer and sacrifice that we can be useful to the Church."

We don't often think that our prayers and sacrifices can do much to help the Church during difficult times, but Thérèse didn't yield to this temptation. She understood that "where sin increased, grace overflowed all the more" (Romans 5:20). What am I doing with the increase of graces God is giving to the faithful during this time? Am I using these graces to pray and suffer for the sake of the Church or just for my own personal interests? Do I need to expand the reach of my prayers to include the good of the Church and the world?

Dear Thérèse, you prayed for souls regardless of whether you saw the fruits of your labor. Help me to exercise the same faith and hope in God who said "the fervent prayer of a righteous person is very powerful" (James 5:16) and pray for the good of the Church.

March 16

"I have my weaknesses also, but I rejoice in them. I don't always succeed either in rising above the nothings of this earth; for example, I will be tormented by a foolish thing I said or did. Then I enter into myself and I say: Alas, I'm still at the same place as I was formerly! It's so good to feel that one is weak and little!"

Thérèse never put on airs, not even to herself! She knew who she was and accepted herself, even though at times she had to struggle to do so. What circumstances cause me to lose patience with myself? Is there a particular fault that I find difficult to accept? Do I need to entrust this fault to God and ask Him to help me be more patient as I struggle to cooperate with the grace He's giving me to overcome it?

Dearest Thérèse, if only I could be as accepting of myself as you were! I see so much wrong in myself that it's hard to keep from becoming discouraged. Please intercede for me that I might receive – and cooperate with – the grace to love myself in spite of my faults.

March 17

*"Never cast little faded flowers ...
only little flowers freshly blooming."*

❧

Thérèse didn't believe in short-changing the Lord, especially when it came to the sufferings she offered. Whether it was in joy or in sorrow, she always gave Him the best of herself. Do I sometimes short-change the Lord in my penances and other Lenten practices by performing them half-heartedly or out of habit?

❧

St. Thérèse, help me to pick only the freshest bouquet of sacrifices to offer to the Lord today.

March 18

*"We must sweeten our minds by charitable thoughts.
After that, the practice of patience will
become almost natural."*

❦

Thérèse gives good advice for those who are trying to be more patient with others during this Lenten season. She knew that when we focus on our neighbor's good points rather than look for things to criticize them about, it's much easier to be patient with them. How can I take Thérèse advice in my daily life today?

❦

Dear Thérèse, my mind is too often filled with thoughts about others that do not reflect Jesus' admonition to "love your neighbor as yourself" (Matt 22:39). Intercede for me that I might repent of these unkind thoughts that too often influence my behavior in a negative way. Help me to make amends by "taking every thought captive in obedience to Christ" (2 Cor 10:5).

March 19

"How many times did others make complaints to good St. Joseph! How many times did they refuse to pay him for his work! Oh! How astonished we would be if we only knew how much they had to suffer!"

On this Feast of St. Joseph, it's good to reflect upon the fact that Joseph endured much of the same sufferings in his everyday life that we experience – the lack of gratitude for work well done, the injustice of being denied the payment he was due, being looked down upon because of his poverty. How is he a model of how a Christian should respond to the crosses and sufferings of life. How might I honor him today by imitating his virtues?

St. Thérèse, intercede for me before the great St. Joseph and ask him to give me the patience to bear the slights of others with grace and peace.

March 20

*"How few there are who do everything
in the best way possible!"*

With the Lenten season dragging on, it's easy to grow tired of the effort. Thérèse certainly felt the same fatigue from time to time during the long and arduous fasts of the cloister; but instead of lessening the intensity, she lifted her arms to God and asked for His help to maintain her fervor. What do I do when I feel the fervor of Lent fade? Do I decrease my devotions, or ask God to lend me His strength to combat the temptation to relax my efforts?

St. Thérèse, you were a little soul just like me and were often left wearied by the struggle, but you never let these moments get the best of you. Instead, you used them as a reminder of your littleness and how much you needed the grace of God. Help me to do the same with my weak moments this Lent, and not be ashamed to ask God for the help I need to continue.

March 21

"If I have nothing but pure suffering, if the heavens are so black that I see no break in the clouds, well, I make this my joy."

Thérèse knew how to find the silver lining in even the darkest moments of her life. This was because her spiritual vision was able to penetrate the blackness and discern the will of God at work – a truth that always brought her joy. Am I able to see the hand of God in the darker moments of life, and to realize that no matter how bad is the suffering of the moment, it is being permitted by God who is in control and knows exactly what I can manage?

Dearest Thérèse, please ask God to increase in me the Holy Spirit's gift of understanding so that I might develop a new spiritual vision that is guided by faith and confidence in His love for me.

March 22

*"When God wills that we be deprived of something,
there is nothing we can do about it;
we must be content to go this way."*

It's not easy to accept the loss of something – or someone – that we hold dear. Thérèse was just a child when she lost her mother and suffered terribly when her father's health declined and he passed away later in her life. In spite of her anguish, she saw everything and everyone in her life as a gift lent to her by God and accepted these painful losses when it was time to return them. How do I behave after a difficult loss? Do I see everything in life – my possessions, my loved ones – as being a gift from God that is just "on loan" and that I may one day have to give back? Do I understand that I will never achieve authentic poverty of spirit until I accept this fundamental truth?

St. Thérèse, lend me some of the courage you showed while suffering through the many painful losses in your life. Help me to understand that everything and everyone I value in life is a gift from God that I must be willing to return should He ask it of me.

March 23

"…I'd be glad to bear the greatest sufferings when this would be for the purpose of making Him smile only once."

Thérèse was always thinking of the One she loved, never herself. The thought of giving God pleasure made every suffering worthwhile. Can I perform my Lenten practices today just for the sake of making God smile?

Dear Little Flower, you loved Jesus with a tender and filial affection that always made you more mindful of Him than of yourself. Intercede for me that I might acquire this same familiar affection for God so that I too may live to please Him.

March 24

"What would happen to me if God didn't give me courage?"

To be courageous doesn't mean to have no fear; it means not letting fear stop you. As Thérèse's illness progressed, she knew it would only become worse, and her humanness naturally felt some fear. But she countered this with faith, knowing that when those difficult moments arrived, He would be right there with her, giving her all the graces she would need to get through the moment. When I'm dreading something, do I give way to fear, or do I cling to my faith and take comfort in knowing that God will never test me beyond my strength?

St. Thérèse, please ask God to give me the grace of supernatural courage, the kind that feels fear, but doesn't let it dim the light of the faith that I hold dear.

March 25

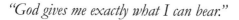

"God gives me exactly what I can bear."

Little souls are often surprised at how much the Lord might ask of them from time to time, be it in the form of sufferings, temptations, or tests of virtue. Thérèse's Little Way has the perfect explanation for this – confidence in God. This is what enables the small and the weak to know that every cross God sends them is perfectly measured to fit them, and in this truth they find their peace. Can I find peace in my trials because I know these crosses were chosen exclusively for me? Do I need to pray for an increase in the virtue of hope today so that I might acquire more confidence in the faithfulness of God?

Dear Thérèse, you were a little soul, but your ability to hope in God made you a giant – even in your littleness! I know that "I have the strength for everything through Him who empowers me" (Phil 4:13) but I need the courage to live this truth. Please pray for me!

93

March 26

"I am content to suffer because God wills it."

Because of her confidence in God and the virtue of hope that enabled her to believe in God's faithfulness with all of her heart, Thérèse knew that whatever God willed for her would invariably turn out for her good. She needed to do nothing more than accept it. Can I honestly say that I accept God's will no matter how it might manifest, or is my acceptance conditional? What makes me hesitate to submit to God's will – fear of suffering, of the unknown, of what might happen to my life if I give it to God?

Dearest Thérèse, your Little Way teaches weak souls to abandon themselves to the will of the God Who loves them. I'm a little soul, but I sometimes hesitate in giving myself so generously to God. What will become of me, my dreams, my future? Please ask God to give me the grace to understand that the key to my happiness is to surrender to His plans for me which are far better than any I could ever achieve on my own.

March 27

"When we accept our disappointment at our failures,
God immediately returns to us."

Thérèse knew that refusing to accept our limitations is a form of pride which results in blocking the grace we might otherwise rely upon to surmount our weakness. Am I trying too hard to advance spiritually on my own? Do I react harshly to myself when I fail? How might I be gentler with myself in my shortcomings today?

St. Thérèse, don't let me stand in the way of the very grace I need to lift me up the steep staircase of perfection. Pray for me to stop trying to do it myself so that I might accept the help the Lord wants to give me – if I will just get out of His way!

March 28

*"You must become gentle; never any harsh words, never
a harsh tone; never take on
a harsh look, always be gentle."*

There were certain nuns in the convent of Lisieux
who tried Thérèse sorely with their irritating habits
and eccentric ways, but she fought with herself to
never let them see her annoyance. How might I
imitate her today?

*St. Thérèse, please pray for me that I might be more gentle and loving
toward the people God allows to come into my life. May everyone
who encounters me today walk away feeling loved and appreciated.*

March 29

"As long as you are humble, you will be happy."

❧

To be humble means to accept who we truly are – creatures of God who are dependent upon Him for our very lives. The only way to achieve this level of humility is to have confidence in God upon Whom we depend. Do I comprehend what it means to be a creature wholly dependent upon God for my very existence? How does this truth make me feel? What does this reaction reveal about my confidence in God?

❧

Dear Thérèse, I find it almost terrifying to be so dependent upon a God Whom I cannot see. When I ponder this, I am assailed with doubts about His mercy and faithfulness. Pray for me that I might come to a full understanding of both my littleness and the love with which God brought me into existence.

❧

On this day in 1875, at the age of three, Thérèse said for the first time that she wanted to be a religious.

March 30

"I am very happy to have no consolation for thus my love is not like that of the world's brides who are always looking at their bridegroom's hands to see if they bear a gift or at his face in the hope of glimpsing a smile of love to enchant them."

This quote explains how Thérèse was able to endure years of aridity in prayer, during which time she felt barely a drop of consolation from the God Whom she loved with all of her heart; but this plight only served to purify her love for Him. Instead of loving Him for the pleasure it might bring to herself, she loved Him for the pleasure she could bring to Him. When my prayer feels dry, do I abandon or shorten it, or do I press on out of love for God?

St. Thérèse, I'm still very attached to my senses and too often let them "guide" me in my spiritual life. Please ask God to help me to learn how to love Him with my will rather than my senses, so that I will remain faithful to Him in good times and in bad.

March 31

"There isn't anyone here more mistrustful of her feelings than I am. I never rely on my own ideas; I know how weak I am."

Thérèse knew that it was a fool's folly to judge the state of our spiritual lives by anything as undependable and fickle as our natural feelings. How often do I evaluate how "good" my prayer is by how much consolation I experienced? Do I believe that the absence of consolations indicates that my prayer was displeasing to God? Do I understand that consolations are a gift from God and not something I can earn?

Thérèse, help me to understand that as my spiritual life progresses, the less my senses can be used as a reliable gauge of my progress. Pray for me that I might learn how to detach from my feelings and rely on faith alone.

REFLECTIONS

FOR

April

April 1

"I'll wait as long as God wills."

Sometimes God's will is to make us wait for Him to respond. Thérèse knew this and was so focused on doing His will that she put aside her own will in order to give deference to His. How patient am I when my prayer requests are not answered right away? What graces do I need to ask for in order to make my will more submissive to God's?

Little Flower, you turned to God for all of your needs, but you were more than willing to wait for Him to respond in the way, and at the time, of His own choosing. Please ask God to give me the grace to do the same!

April 2

"I've acted just like a warrior who, hearing himself always being praised for his bravery, and knowing that he's nothing but a coward, ends up by being ashamed of the compliments and wants to be deserving of them."

It's so easy to take credit for what we don't deserve – but sincerely wish we did! The Little Way teaches us to be content to give the credit to God and not be ashamed of who we are – little souls whose only hope of greatness rests in God alone. What successes in life has God enabled me to achieve? Have I thanked Him for His help?

Dearest Thérèse, pray for me that I might be a warrior like you who is fully aware of all the credit God deserves for the good He enables me to do!

On this night in 1896, Thérèse received the first hemoptysis in her cell indicating the presence of tuberculosis in her lungs.

April 3

"I always see the good side of things."

Even though she suffered through periods of illness, scruples, and tragic personal losses, Thérèse always looked on the bright side. This is because she kept her eyes on Jesus and didn't dare to look down lest she sink into the darkness. How do I handle the dark moments of my life? Do I strive to keep my eyes focused on Jesus or do I let myself be consumed by self-pity or despair? Can I find something good to celebrate in the darkest areas of my life? How does this reflect the face of Jesus to me?

St. Thérèse, rather than focus on the negative, please help me to concentrate on the good in others, in the world around me, and in myself, so that I might better perceive the comforting presence of Christ.

April 4

"Jesus is thirsting more than ever for love."

Thérèse was devoted to loving God, so much so that she desired to spend her eternity making Him more loved. God showers us with His loving care every day of our lives, and yet receives not even fraction in return. How many acts of love for God can I pack into this day?

St. Thérèse, pray for me that my heart might catch fire for love of God so that I will never let a day go by without showing Him how much I love Him.

April 5

"I expect as much from God's justice as from His mercy. It is because He is just that 'He is compassionate and filled with gentleness, slow to punish and abundant in mercy,' for He knows our frailty. He remembers that we are only dust. As a father has tenderness for his children, so the Lord has compassion on us."

❦

This quote, from a letter written by Thérèse to Father Adolphe Roulland in 1897, gives us an excellent explanation of Thérèse's approach to the justice of God – an approach that was at the root of her great confidence in God. She saw Him as a father full of compassion who understands the weakness of His children, and takes these weaknesses into account when doling out punishment. Do I see God as a father who understands my frailty, or as a demanding and harsh judge? Does Thérèse's approach to God's justice inspire me with more confidence in God?

❦

Dear Little Flower, intercede for me that I might receive the grace to see God for Who He truly is, a loving Father who cares for me, rather than a harsh taskmaster. Help me to put aside these false notions of God and let Him teach me a new way to know Him – and to love Him!

April 6

"My way is all confidence and love."

❧

Having reflected on yesterday's quote explaining how Thérèse regarded God's justice, do I understand why she would claim that the Little Way was "all confidence and love." Am I ready to make her Little Way *my* Little Way?

❧

St. Thérèse, you have opened my eyes to a whole new way of regarding God and it is inspiring me with the same confidence and love that you felt for Him during your life. Ask God to help me to continue to cooperate with the graces He is sending me to make your Little Way my Little Way!

April 7

*"What does it matter what others think or say?
I don't see why I should be disturbed about it."*

❦

Thérèse was not concerned about what other people thought of her because God's opinion was all that mattered. How swayed am I by the opinion of others? Whose opinion matters the most to me in life? How much does God's opinion really matter to me?

❦

Dear Thérèse, I'm too often more concerned about my reputation in the eyes of others than I am about God's opinion of me. Pray for me that I might have the grace to overcome my need for human respect and aim to please God first and foremost.

April 8

"Everything outside of God is vanity."

Even though she openly admitted to having been a spoiled child, Thérèse was not egotistical or selfish. Thérèse exemplified spiritual simplicity in how she made God the center of her universe and the object of her desire. Although she loved her family fiercely, God was always first. Where is God on my list of important people? Do I regard my relationship with Him to be the most important relationship of my life? What relationships come before Him?

St. Thérèse, please pray for me that I might simplify my interior life and learn how to do everything for God's sake – loving my family, caring for their needs, being a good friend, remaining faithful to my vocation in life, serving the Church, etc. Pray that I might learn how to do all for God!

April 9

*"When I commit a fault that makes me sad …
I hasten to say to God: My God, I know I have
merited this feeling of sadness, but let me offer it up to
You just the same as a trial that You sent me through
love. I'm sorry for my sin, but I'm happy to
have this suffering to offer to You."*

❦

Even when she fell and had nothing more than sorrow for her sin, Thérèse found something beautiful to offer to God. Have I ever thought to offer God the suffering my own faults cause me? How can I use this suffering as reparation for my sins, and the sins of the world?

❦

St. Thérèse, I get so wrapped up in my own disappointment after a fall that I don't even think to make an offering of this suffering to God. Help me to move beyond the shame so that I can offer my sorrow to God in reparation for those who sin repeatedly and without regret.

❦

On this day in 1888, Thérèse entered the Carmel of Lisieux. She was 15-years-old.

April 10

"You will not arrive at what you desire by following your own path, or even by high contemplation; but only through a great humility and a surrender of the heart."

❧

Thérèse knew that it is only when a soul experiences its own limitations, and realizes the loving power of the One who calls it to sanctity, that it can truly let go and let God. What holds me back from this surrender? Is it a lack of self-knowledge, or insufficient confidence in the loving power of God – or both?

❧

Dear Thérèse, you knew that the truly humble soul is a surrendered soul. I want to surrender to God but I'm still prone to self-reliance and lack of trust in God. Ask God to give me the courage to see the truth about myself – and Him – so that I can let Him lead me from this day forward.

April 11

"Joy isn't found in the material objects surrounding us but in the inner recesses of the soul. One can possess joy in a prison cell as well as in a palace."

Like so many saints before her, Thérèse understood that one cannot achieve true joy without first achieving peace of soul. When the heart is right with God, everything else falls in place. Do I find my joy in God, or do I seek it in the "things" of the world? What were the happiest moments of my life? Did they concern "things" or people or God?

St. Thérèse, please ask God to give me the grace to rid my soul of any darkness that weighs me down and causes me to look for happiness in all the wrong places.

April 12

"How can I fear one whom I love so much?"

As Thérèse knew, "There is no fear in love, but perfect love drives out fear because fear has to do with punishment and so one who fears is not yet perfect in love" (1 John 4: 18). Thérèse was convinced of God's mercy and did not fear punishment from Him because even His reprimands were cloaked in love. Can I say the same? Do I secretly fear punishment from God for my past sins or my current failures?

St. Thérèse, please intercede for me that God might give me the grace to move beyond my fears and acquire the perfect love for God that He deserves.

April 13

"It took me a long time before I was established in this degree of abandonment. Now I am there; God has placed me there. He took me into His arms and placed me there."

❦

Thérèse's spiritual heroics impressed everyone but herself. Yes, she was utterly abandoned to God, but not because of anything she did. It was all due to God Who decided the right time to grant her the grace of true surrender. Do I realize that the same grace is available to me? Am I ready to ask for it today?

❦

St. Thérèse, I can only imagine the kind of peace a person will feel who is totally abandoned to God! Pray for me that I might have the courage to ask for this grace — and to cooperate with it whenever God might choose to grant it.

April 14

"I love only simplicity; I have a horror for pretense."

❧

Thérèse had no time for duplicity. She behaved as Jesus directed when He said, "Let your 'yes' mean 'yes' and your 'no' mean 'no.' Everything else is from the evil one" (Matthew 5:37). Being a simple soul, she always said what she meant. Do I sometimes say things I don't mean just to please others or to "keep the peace?" How straightforward am I in my dealings with others? Is this weakness something I need to take to prayer?

❧

Little Flower, help me to find the courage to be who I am and not resort to deception in order to protect myself or my reputation. Ask God to give me the grace to put pleasing Him above pleasing myself or others.

April 15

"You go to too much trouble over things that aren't worth any trouble."

Thérèse was never one to waste time with trivial pursuits. Everything about her was purposeful and directed toward her main aim in life – to please God. Am I easily led into aimless conversations or activities that waste time, upset me, or lead me away from God? What extraneous activities might I consider giving up in order to live a more recollected and contemplative life?

St. Thérèse, help me to be as decisive as you when it comes to filling the hours of my day. Pray that I might avoid idleness or any activities that dissipate the life of my soul so that I might remain clear-eyed and focused on pleasing God.

April 16

"God alone can understand me."

❦

We all have someone in our life who understands us like no other. In Thérèse's life, this person was God. She felt as close to Him as we feel to our spouse or sibling or best friend. These kinds of close relationships can only come about through an investment of time and attention. How much time do I spend every day in prayer to God? Is it focused, quality time, or do I pray when I'm doing something else like driving or vacuuming? Do I need to make some adjustments to my prayer life so that my friendship with God can become more intimate?

❦

St. Thérèse, I want to be as close to God as you were. Pray for me that I might open my heart to Him like never before, to hold nothing back and tell Him everything, so that He might become the one friend who knows me like no other.

April 17

*"One could believe that it is because I haven't sinned
that I have such great confidence in God…
if I had committed all possible crimes, I would always
have the same confidence; I feel that
this whole multitude of offenses would be like
a drop of water thrown into a fiery furnace."*

Perhaps Thérèse knew that after her death, people would say, "Of course Thérèse was confident in God – she never sinned!" But, as we recently learned, her confidence wasn't founded on herself – it was founded on her trust in His Fatherly love. As I slowly begin to grow in confidence, what adjustments need to be made to my image of God as a loving Father? Has a less-than-perfect father made it difficult for me to embrace God as a father? Do I need healing in order to fully enjoy the paternal love of God for me?

Little Flower, I'm a sinner who has fallen many times and experienced God's loving forgiveness over and over again. Pray for me that I might receive the grace to forgive and to heal – and to realize that God is the only perfect Father!

April 18

"I hold nothing in my hands. Everything I have,
everything I merit is for the Church and for souls.
If I were to live to eighty, I will always be
as poor as I am now."

People spend their entire lives trying to acquire things. Thérèse was just the opposite. She spent her life trying to lose all so that she could stand before God with empty hands, having nothing to boast about before Him Whose grace made her who she was. What emotions are inspired in me when I imagine standing before God with empty hands? Does this make me nervous, fearful, anxious? What does this tell me about my level of confidence in God?

Dearest Thérèse, help me to accept the fact that I'm still very self-reliant when it comes to the spiritual life. I think I have to do this or that in order to merit God's approval, but you teach the exact opposite. Holiness is a grace with which I have to cooperate, and it is only then that I will acquire the confidence to stand before God with empty hands.

April 19

"Ah! How blessed we are to be able to laugh at everything...Oh! Yes! There is no but for that..."

Thérèse always had a sense of humor, even during the last days of her life. Her ready wit was a source of great amusement to the sisters during recreation time at Lisieux. It's important to note that the words "humor" and "humble" start with the same three letters – and for good reason. Only the truly humble know how to laugh at themselves. Do I take myself too seriously sometimes? Am I able to laugh at my faults and foibles even as I work to correct them?

St. Thérèse, laughter is so refreshing! Help me lighten up!

April 20

"Whenever I involuntarily caused anyone any trouble, I would beg God to repair it, and then I no longer tormented myself with the matter."

We all experience times when we accidentally cause someone pain. Even though we didn't intend to do so, we can sometimes be very slow to forgive ourselves. Thérèse had a healthy self-esteem and never wasted time blaming herself for things she didn't mean to do. She preferred to stay focused on her real faults rather than torment herself over unintentional mistakes. After apologizing and asking God to help repair the damage, she put the matter behind her. How do I react when I accidentally hurt someone? Do I ruminate on the mistake, going over and over it in my mind, making myself feel even worse, or do I accept the episode as an unfortunate mistake, give it to God, and move on?

St. Thérèse, help me to be more understanding with myself when I accidentally cause hurt or damage. Pray for me that I will be humble enough to acknowledge my mistakes.

April 21

"God made me always desire what He wanted to give me."

❦

In the Little Way, surrender to God's will is everything, and the easiest way to achieve this is to ask God to change our hearts so that we will want whatever He wants. By doing so, His desires become our desires and, therefore, we are never disappointed! Have I ever asked God to "change my heart" so that it might be filled with His desires? What desires fill my heart today? How many of them are Godly desires? Will today be the day to ask Him for this favor?

❦

Dearest Thérèse, asking God to fill my heart with His own desires is just another one of those clever shortcuts you built into the Little Way to assist little souls like me to achieve the sanctity God has planned for me. Pray that I will let go of any desires that I can't share with Him!

April 22

"How necessary it is for a person to be detached from and elevated above herself in order not to experience any harm."

Although we hardly notice it, we're all attached to ourselves in one way or another – to our opinions, our habits, our comforts, our possessions – and these attachments are often what lead us to sin. Even worse, Thérèse knew from the readings of one of her favorite saints, St. John of the Cross, that these attachments are like mud on the window of our souls, preventing the full light of God's grace to penetrate. What am I most attached to about myself? Is this something that leads me toward – or away – from God? Do I need to pray for the grace to begin to sever this attachment?

St. Thérèse, please ask God to open my eyes that I might see all the attachments that are keeping me chained to myself. I want to let go of my egotistical ways so that I can make room in my heart for more love for God and others.

April 23

"Why fear in advance? Wait at least for it to happen before having any distress."

Like so many spiritual masters before and after her, Thérèse understood the great damage that can be done to our interior life by giving in to anxious forethought. Because she knew that God exists only in the present, this was the only place she wanted to be! Do I prudently prepare for the future, then return to the present moment and leave the rest to God, or do I dwell on it and allow myself to become anxious about it? Is this something I need to take to prayer today.

Dearest Thérèse, I know that being anxious about the future means that I'm not trusting in God the way I should. Show me how to avoid "crossing the line" between prudent preparation for the future, and trying to control the future that belongs to God.

April 24

"I'm a little seed; no one knows yet what will develop."

Until the last days of her life, Thérèse was continually learning and growing in her faith. She was perfectly open to being a "little seed" that God would develop in whatever way He desired. Am I open to growth in the Lord, or do I try to direct own spiritual growth? Am I willing to become the saint God has in mind for me, or do I have my own ideas about the kind of saint I ought to be?

St. Thérèse, thank you for reminding me that my sanctity will be God's doing, not my own. The only thing I can take credit for is being willing to grow from the "little seed" He planted to the flower He aims to produce. Ask God to give me the grace to be willing to become the saint He wants me to be!

April 25

"God allows Himself to be represented by whomever He wills."

❧

Little souls are sometimes so overwhelmed by their own weakness they forget that God "chose the weak of the world to shame the strong" (1 Cor 1:27). Thérèse was very well aware of this truth and never hesitated to offer herself for His purposes, knowing that He would qualify her to represent Him as He deserved. Does my fear of being "unqualified" prevent me from serving God in my home, my parish, or the world? Am I forgetting that "those He called He also justified" (Romans 8:30)?

❧

Dearest Thérèse, help me to understand how prideful it is for me to decline to serve God because I feel "unqualified." Although it sounds humble, it actually disguises a hidden reliance on oneself rather than in God's help. Pray for me that I might overcome this tendency in myself and offer myself to God as courageously as you did!

April 26

"Mortal sin wouldn't withdraw my confidence from me."

Trusting in the fathomless mercy of God, Thérèse was confident that as long as we are sincerely sorry, God will forgive anything. What sins has God forgiven me in the past and what does this tell me about His mercy? How does this affect my confidence in Him?

St. Thérèse, help me to know that I need not run away in shame from God over my sins. Instead, I need to run toward Him and take shelter in His loving embrace.

April 27

"Persecution has changed in form; the apostles of Christ have not changed in sentiment."

⬥

She might have lived her life in a cloister, but Thérèse understood persecution much better than most of us. She experienced the same bloodless persecution so prevalent in our time – the mockery of Christian beliefs, the stripping of prayer from schools and public places, the denigration of the Judeo-Christian moral code.   But today, just as in her time, the followers of Christ still love Him as much as ever! How does the persecution of Christians impact me in my daily life? How do I respond to it?

⬥

St. Thérèse, help me to pray for my persecutors and to never forget what Jesus promised to those who suffer for His sake, "for their reward will be great in heaven" (Matt 5: 11).

April 28

"I have never attached any importance to the opinion of creatures, and this impression has so developed in me that, at this present time, reproaches and compliments glide over me without leaving the slightest imprint."

Imagine how peaceful it would be if we could be so immune to the opinions of others! Thérèse could do so because her Little Way focuses on the One Whose opinion matters most of all – and everyone else's naturally pales by comparison. How impacted am I to the opinion of others? Do I try to please everyone? Am I overly-sensitive and too easily offended? Is this because of some inner woundedness that I need to take to God today?

Little Flower, pray for me that I will not get so distracted by the opinion of others, especially if this makes me overlook the opinion that should always matter most – God's.

April 29

"I'm not an egoist; it's God whom I love, not myself!"

❧

Thérèse had a healthy self-esteem, but she was no egoist. She was too busy loving God to get that wrapped up in herself. In a culture that idolizes individualism, in what ways has this made me selfish? Have I become so focused on "being me" that I lose sight of God and the person He created me to be? Is something I need to address with God in prayer?

❧

Dear Thérèse, help me to put my uniqueness to work for God and His Kingdom here on earth, rather than for myself.

❧

On this day in 1923, Thérèse was beatified by Pope Pius XI.

April 30

"*I'm tired of this earth! We receive compliments when
we don't merit them, and reproaches when
we don't merit them, either.*"

❧

Life can be so unfair! Thérèse experienced injustice
during her life but learned how to make an offering
of these sufferings to God in expiation for the sins
of those who perpetrate unfairness. Are there some
areas in my life where I am too judgmental? How do I
treat those who do not share my Catholic worldview?
Do I need to repent of any form of discrimination?

❧

*Thérèse, you prayed with as much fervor for atheists and
condemned criminals as you did your family and fellow sisters
in Carmel. Ask God to give me the grace to resist the urge to
judge others so that I might treat everyone as a child worthy
of God's love.*

REFLECTIONS

FOR

May

May 1

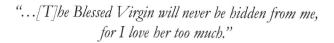

"…[T]he Blessed Virgin will never be hidden from me, for I love her too much."

❧

Thérèse always had the same childlike confidence in Mary that she had in God. She truly believed that because Mary was her Mother, She would always be there for her. As we begin this month devoted to Our Lady, this is the perfect time to assess our own relationship with Our Lady. How confident am I in her love for me? How does that love impact my life of faith? How often do I turn to her during the day to seek her guidance and protection?

❧

St. Thérèse, please intercede for me that I might use this special time of year to grow in love for the Mother of God.

May 2

"Asking the Blessed Virgin for something is not the same thing as asking God. She really knows what is to be done about my little desires, whether or not she must speak about them to God. So it's up to her to see that God is not forced to answer me, to allow Him to do everything He pleases."

Our Lady can do nothing outside of God's will and Thérèse had no problem with this! However, this doesn't make Mary any less formidable as an intercessor before God. Do I understand Our Lady's role as an intercessor before God, that She is not detracting from God but pointing toward Him? How often do I rely on Her intercession for my daily needs?

St. Thérèse, there were many special moments between you and Our Lady during your life such as when you were miraculously healed after prayer in front of a statue of Our Lady, and when She provided critical comfort to you in your final illness. Please pray for me that I too will enjoy many special moments with Mary and me during my lifetime.

May 3

"The Blessed Virgin doesn't have a Blessed Virgin to love, and so she's less happy than we are."

❦

As endearing as this statement sounds, it gives important insight into the depth of Thérèse's devotion to Our Lady. Having such a quintessential Mother to love was a source of happiness for Thérèse. Can I say the same?

❦

Little Flower, you lost your mother at the age of four and although your sisters tried hard to fill her place, no one did this better than Our Lady. Pray for me that I might take Mary as my Mother today and live the rest of my life rejoicing in Her presence in my life.

May 4

"When I think of how much trouble I've had all my life trying to recite the Rosary!"

Thérèse never hid the fact that she struggled to pray the Rosary. No matter how hard she tried, it was always more of a loving labor than a peaceful prayer – but that didn't stop her from praying it! Have I responded to Our Lady's request to pray the Rosary? Do I let my struggles with distraction during recitation of the Rosary discourage me from praying it? Do I need to ask Her to help me to persevere in this holy practice?

St. Thérèse, praying the Rosary can sometimes be hard, and I don't often do it well, but I pray it because Our Lady asked me too, and that's enough reason for me. Please ask Mary to intercede for me that I might continue to offer this powerful prayer for the conversion of sinners and peace in the world.

May 5

"How I would have loved to be a priest in order to preach about the Blessed Virgin!"

Although this quote is often taken out of context and made to sound as if Thérèse endorsed women's ordination, this was never her intention. Thérèse simply admired Mary so much that she wanted a chance to tell the world about Her. If I had the opportunity to preach a sermon on Our Lady, what would I say? What attributes of Our Lady would I celebrate in my sermon?

St. Thérèse, intercede for me that I might have a heart that loves and admires Mary like yours did — and that I might have the courage to proclaim Her whenever the opportunity arises!

May 6

"For a sermon on the Blessed Virgin to please me and do me any good, I must see her real life, not her imagined life."

Thérèse had no patience for flowery descriptions of Our Lady that placed Her on a pedestal so high that She could barely be reached by the faithful. Instead, Thérèse wanted the "real" Mary, a woman who lived and worked and prayed like she did. Have I placed Mary on a pedestal in my spiritual life? Do I regard imitation of Her as a possibility for me, or as an unattainable goal?

Thérèse, help me to bring Mary "down to earth" where I can relate to Her as a woman, a wife, and a mother. Ask God to give me the grace to overcome any hesitation I might have about imitating Her immaculate virtues.

May 7

"We know very well that the Blessed Virgin is Queen of heaven and earth; but she is more Mother than Queen."

Thérèse would never strip the crown Our Lady so richly deserved, but she refused to let it obscure who She truly was – a mother *par excellence.* How do I regard the various roles of Our Lady – Mother of God, Mother of the faithful, Queen of Heaven and Earth? Which one am I most attracted to? Why?

St. Thérèse, pray for me that I might acquire the childlike love for our Mother Mary that you had while you lived upon the earth.

May 8

"When we pray to the Blessed Virgin and she doesn't answer, that's a sign she doesn't want to. Then it's better to leave her alone and not torment ourselves."

Thérèse understood that the Blessed Virgin Mary was completely surrendered to the will of God and knew that when Mary did not answer a request, it was because this was God's will. For this reason, she always bowed her head in submission and let the matter drop. How well do I understand that Mary remains the "handmaid of God" even in eternity, and that She is unable to grant any wish that does not comply with God's will? Do I sometimes go to Mary because I think She can "twist God's arm" and allow me to get what I want?

Thérèse, help me to understand that going to Jesus through Mary is an act of humility on my part. It acknowledges the fact that I'm a sinner and that God may be more likely to answer my plea if He hears it voiced through the lips of His immaculate Mother. But even this doesn't guarantee how my prayer will be answered. Pray for me that I may learn how to accept "no" for an answer without becoming discouraged.

On this day in 1884, Thérèse received her First Holy Communion.

May 9

"O my good Blessed Virgin, take pity on me!"

❦

Thérèse uttered this plea on one of the last days of her life when she was in so much pain that she could hardly bear another minute of it. Although she accepted the pain and made a gift of the suffering to the Lord, she was not too proud to cry out to Our Lady for help to endure. When I am pushed to the brink of my tolerance, am I reluctant to ask for help because I'm trying to impress God or to "soldier on?"

❦

Little Flower, help me to understand that it's okay for little souls like me to ask Our Lady for help, even when I'm suffering for God and "offering it up". Pray for me that I might not lose sight of my littleness and try to be braver than I really am.

May 10

"Who could ever invent the Blessed Virgin?"

Contemplating the virtues of Mary can leave one awestruck, and Thérèse was no different, but she was also able to see the brilliance of God in Mary's perfection. What does the creation of the sinless Virgin Mary say to me about the mind and heart of God?

St. Thérèse, you saw the hand of God in everything and everyone — especially in the creation of His Mother. Pray for me that I might behold the glories of God as revealed in Mary, and in everyone I encounter today!

May 11

"Virgin Mary, I love you with all my heart!"

It was not in the least bit difficult for Thérèse to love both heavenly and earthly beings and she did so with all of her heart. Our Lady, the saints, the angels, were as real to her as her sisters in Carmel. How close do I feel to Our Lord and Our Lady? Do I find it difficult to relate to them because they are not of this world? How close is my relationship to my guardian angel?

Dearest Thérèse, please ask God to open the eyes of my heart so that I might behold by faith what I cannot see with my natural vision, thus enabling me to draw closer to Him and all of my friends in heaven.

May 12

"The Blessed Virgin is my mother, and little children ordinarily resemble their mother."

At first sight, this might sound like Thérèse was handing herself a backhanded compliment, but she was merely stating a fact – children normally resemble their mother. Because of this, if someone saw anything to admire in her soul, it was because she was reflecting the qualities of the Mother of God. In what ways do I resemble my mother, Mary? Do I need to pay more attention to reflecting Her qualities in my life?

St. Thérèse, you identified so strongly with being a child of Mary that you attributed your own beauty to Her. Help me to be more mindful of imitating Our Lady in my daily life so that I might reflect Her beauty to the world around me.

May 13

"When we ask a grace from the Blessed Virgin, we receive immediate help. Have you not experienced this? Well, try it and you will see."

❧

Our Lady is always anxious to grant graces to Her children. Thérèse was so aware of her own limitations that she was never too shy to ask for the graces she needed to achieve the sainthood she desired. What graces should I ask Mary for today? Should I also ask her to grant me the grace to *cooperate* with those graces?

❧

St. Thérèse, your great confidence in Our Lady inspires me to turn to Her with the same childlike confidence as you did. Pray for me that I might develop a holy habit of turning to Mary for all of the graces I need to become the saint God wants me to be.

❧

On this day in 1883, which was the Feast of Pentecost, Thérèse was miraculously healed of a mysterious illness after seeing a statue of Our Lady smile.

May 14

"The Blessed Virgin never fails to protect me as soon as I invoke her. In my troubles and anxieties, I very quickly turn toward her and, like the most tender of mothers, she always takes care of my interests."

Our world is full of physical and spiritual dangers and Our Lady has been the refuge of untold numbers of souls, including St. Thérèse, over the centuries. What do I need protection from today – a particular temptation, a weakness, a fear? Have I asked Our Lady for her help?

St. Thérèse, please intercede for me that I might turn more readily to Mary for her help in all the difficulties of my life, knowing that this tender mother will always take care of my best interests.

May 15

"I like to hide my pains from the good Lord, because I want to give Him the impression that I am always happy, but I hide nothing from the Blessed Virgin: to her I tell everything."

Of course the Lord knew all that Thérèse was trying to hide from Him, but He also saw that this sentiment came from a desire to make Him happy. This gesture certainly pleased Our Lady's Immaculate Heart as well! What loving gesture can I perform today to please both Jesus – and His Mother?

St. Thérèse, mothers are always happy to see their sons appreciated. Pray that God will give me the grace to show my appreciation for Jesus so that I can make Our Lady smile today!

May 16

"O Mary, if I were Queen of Heaven and you were Thérèse, I would rather become Thérèse, that you might be the Queen of Heaven."

This statement perfectly describes the reverence and genuine filial love with which Thérèse viewed Our Lady. Can I offer Mary this same sweet sentiment by substituting my name in place of Thérèse's? "O Mary, if I (*name*) were Queen of Heaven and you were (*name*), I would rather become (*name*) so that you might be Queen of Heaven."

Dear Thérèse, ask God to grant me the grace to love Mary with the filial love of a child so that loving Her, and emulating Her, will become natural for me.

May 17

"A mother's heart always understands, even when her child can do little more than lisp."

How true this is! Only a mother can understand her child's language even when it sounds like gibberish to everyone else. When I try to enunciate my needs to Our Lady, am I confident that She understands the depth of my heart, or do I think I have to "ask perfectly?" Do I see her as a mother who always understands me? What can I do today to make my relationship with Mary more intimate and trusting?

St. Thérèse, in moments of great anguish, when you could do little more than cry out to Our Lady for help, you knew She heard and understood what you needed. Pray for me that I might develop this kind of deep and personal trust in Her love and concern for me.

On this day in 1925, Thérèse was canonized at St. Peter's in Rome by Pius XI, drawing a crowd of nearly 500,000 pilgrims.

May 18

"The insight of the most skilled doctors can't compare with that of a mother's heart."

For a child who lost her mother at the age of four, Thérèse had remarkable insight about the heart of a mother, much of which she learned from her sisters, but also from her devotion to Our Lady. Hers was a trusting heart that felt free to share confidences with the various mother-figures in her life. Do I regard Our Lady as a close confidant? Do I share my innermost secrets and hopes with Her?

Little Flower, intercede for me that I might invite Mary into my heart and thus develop a closer and more personal relationship with Her.

May 19

"I made up my mind that I must consecrate myself in some special way to Our Lady."

Making an act of consecration takes devotion to a new level because it requires a person to make a formal act of personal dedication. Have I consecrated myself to Mary? If so, how well am I living this consecration? In what way can I improve? Do I understand that any consecration to Mary is actually a consecration to Jesus through Her? If I haven't yet done so, am I ready to ask Thérèse to help me find my own special way to make this consecration in the near future?

Dear Thérèse, guide me in my life of consecration to Mary. Help me to regard this dedication for what it is - a sacred trust between Jesus, Mary and myself.

May 20

*"The sufferings of Jesus pierced the heart of His Mother,
so the sufferings and humiliations of the
ones we love the best on earth pierce ours."*

The most difficult sufferings to endure are usually not our own; they are the sufferings that afflict those we love. How we wish we could take their sufferings upon ourselves and spare them the pain! What sufferings are piercing my own heart in this life? Do I realize that this pain pierces the heart of Jesus and Mary as well as my own? Is this suffering something that might become a powerful act of reparation for my sins, and the sins of my loved ones? Is anything preventing me from making that offering today?

Dearest Thérèse, please plead for me before God that I might have the courage and strength to not only bear my crosses and those that afflict my loved ones, but to offer up the pain in reparation for our offenses.

May 21

*"I think of my soul as a piece of waste ground and ask
Our Lady to take away the rubbish of my imperfections
and then build a spacious tabernacle there, worthy of
Heaven, adorning it with her own loveliness."*

Thérèse used her imagination in her prayer life
in creative ways that always managed to express
the sentiments of her heart even while remaining
grounded in the reality of who she was – a small, weak
soul in need of constant help. What imperfections,
procrastinations, attachments to sin and other
"rubbish" needs to be cleared out of my soul before it
can become a worthy tabernacle of God?

*St. Thérèse, help me to invite Our Lady into my heart today
and ask Her to show me the "rubbish" that needs to be
cleaned from my soul in the Sacrament of Confession.*

May 22

"I take refuge in prayer; I have only to turn to Mary, and Jesus triumphs over everything."

❦

Thérèse understood that every prayer and action we direct toward Our Lady is ultimately directed to Jesus. This is because She always points to Her Son. Do I understand this concept? Do I realize that it's much humbler to go to Jesus through Mary because She cleans away the self-love in our thoughts, thus presenting Him with the kind of pure prayer that He deserves?

❦

St. Thérèse, help me to understand Our Lady and Her role in my salvation better, so that I will no longer hesitate to go to Jesus through Her.

May 23

"The Blessed Virgin is sometimes pictured as if she were unapproachable. We should realize, on the contrary, that it is possible to imitate her by practicing her hidden virtues."

While it's true that Our Lady's perfect virtue was the result of her being born "full of grace," God makes grace available to all of us so that we might not feel as if the imitation of Mary is beyond our capability. How do I really feel about the task of imitating Mary's virtues? Is this something I regard as being impossible for me? Is this because I am secretly relying on myself and forgetting that "For human beings this is impossible, but for God all things are possible" (Matt 19:26)?

Little Flower, don't let me fall into the trap of self-reliance! Help me to always remember that God wouldn't ask me to do anything, such as imitate the virtues of His mother, unless He planned to give me the grace to do so. Help me to ask for the grace, and to cooperate with it to the best of my ability.

May 24

"With regard to the Blessed Virgin, I must confide to you one of my simple ways with her. I surprise myself at times by saying to her: 'But good Blessed Virgin, I am more blessed than you, for I have you for Mother, and you do not have a Blessed to love.'"

This is yet another vintage Theresian sentiment! Mary was so important to her that she couldn't imagine life without Her – even so far as lamenting that Mary didn't have a "Mary" to love like she did! How important is Mary in my life? Can I imagine what my spiritual life would be without Her?

Little Flower, you loved Mary so much that you wished she could have a Mary too! Pray for me that Mary will become my joy and my consolation in this world, and the next!

May 25

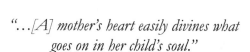

*"...[A] mother's heart easily divines what
goes on in her child's soul."*

A mother's intuition about her child has a way
of discerning what is unseen to the naked eye.
Sometimes she just "knows" what her child is
thinking or feeling without being told. Because
Mary loves me even more than my natural mother,
She will have the same intuition about me if I am
open to sharing myself with Her as a child shares
itself with its mother. Am I ready to do that on a
deeper level today?

*St. Thérèse, help me to draw closer to the ever-faithful and
always-loving Immaculate Heart of Mary so that I can share
my heart with Her more fully from here on.*

May 26

"I do not tremble when I see my weakness, for the treasures of a mother belong also to her child, and I am thy child, O dear Mother Mary."

As this quote reminds us, the source of Thérèse's confidence was never in herself – but always in God and Mary. She trusted that like her Father, her heavenly Mother would also provide whatever she needed to achieve the sanctity God intended for her on earth. Upon whom do I base my confidence in achieving holiness? I may think that I'm relying on God to help me, but do my actions correspond with this desire? Am I still trying to do too much on my own?

St. Thérèse, help me to discern the ways in which I am placing too much confidence in myself and not enough in the God Who makes all things possible for me.

May 27

"*The loveliest masterpiece of the heart of God
is the heart of a mother.*"

Genuine maternal love is probably the closest we humans can come to the pure agape love of Jesus Christ. It is only by the grace of God that we can achieve this standard of love on earth. Whether I am a physical mother, or spiritual mother like Thérèse, in what way do I see the growth of agape love in my heart?

Dearest Little Flower, please ask God to bless me with the selfless love of Jesus Christ so that I can fulfill His request to "love one another as I have loved you" (John 13:34).

May 28

"Our Lady was helping me to prepare a wedding garment for my soul."

Thérèse regarded Mary as a Mother but also as a powerful aid in her spiritual life. She knew that if she commended herself into Our Lady's care, that She would make sure Thérèse's soul was properly prepared to fulfil God's plan for her life. Do I rely on Mary to help me in my spiritual life? How often do I call upon Mary to assist me in my prayer life and in the daily practice of Christian virtue?

St. Thérèse, I want to rely on Our Lady as readily and confidently as you did. Help me to turn to Her often during the day and to entrust my soul to Her without reservation.

May 29

"I felt entirely hidden under the veil of the Blessed Virgin."

A long litany of saints, including Thérèse of Lisieux, attest to the fact that Our Lady is a powerful protectress in both the physical and spiritual life. Where do I need the most protection in my physical life? Have I asked Our Lady to help with this? What dangers do I face in my spiritual life that Mary can help me with today?

St. Thérèse, don't let me hold back from asking Mary for the help I need either because I'm trying to do it myself or I'm afraid of bothering her with "little things." Help me to remember that She's always there, waiting to help me, if only I would ask!

On this day in 1887, which was the Feast of Pentecost, Thérèse received permission from her father to enter Carmel at the age of 15.

May 30

"I felt that the Blessed Virgin was watching over me, that I was her child. Hence, I found it necessary to call her 'Mama,' for this name seemed even more tender than that of a mother."

The Blessed Virgin Mary was like a beloved family member to Thérèse. She not only experienced the maternal love of Mary, but she reciprocated it with the love of a child for its mother. How would I describe my relationship with Mary? Is it close and personal like a mother/child relationship, as a friend, or do I envision her as "unreachable?" What relationship with Mary would I like to have – beginning right now?

Dear Thérèse, I want to come closer to Mary so that I can feel Her comforting, motherly presence in my life. Please ask Jesus to send me whatever graces I need to overcome anything that might be standing in the way of a closer relationship with His Mother.

May 31

"She [Our Lady] already occupied a very large place in my heart, but I promised to give her even more."

❧

There were no half-measures in Thérèse's life. When she gave her heart, she gave all of it, even when this caused heartache such as when she was shunned by a childhood friend during her school years. Can I give more of myself to Mary today? As we say goodbye to this beautiful month in Her honor, how can say "thank you" to Her for all that She's done for me?

❧

St. Thérèse, Mary was like a mother to you and you gave her your heart with the innocent and trusting joy of a child. Ask God to grant me whatever graces I need to give myself to Mary without reserve from this day forward.

REFLECTIONS

FOR

June

June 1

"I kneel before the tabernacle, knowing that I shall learn much more from You in prayer and recollection than in perusing learned books."

❧

Even though Thérèse had limited access to spiritual books, and never had a spiritual director, she remained so close to God in daily prayer that she was still able achieve the height of sanctity. Am I grateful for the plentitude of resources available to help me grow in my faith? How does my spiritual reading impact my prayer life?

❧

St. Thérèse, when I consider how far you traveled in the spiritual life with God as your director, it gives me hope that regardless of whether I have a director, I can achieve sanctity in this world.

June 2

"O sweet, divine Guest, You know my misery; that is why You come to me in the hope of finding an empty tabernacle, a heart wholly emptied of self. This is all You ask."

Thérèse was very devoted to Our Eucharistic Lord, Whom she often referred to as "the Divine Prisoner." When I receive the Lord, do I think of myself as being a tabernacle for Him? How might I make myself more worthy of that description?

St. Thérèse, you were careful to keep your soul pure and spotless so that Jesus would find a comfortable abode in you when He came to you in the Eucharist. Pray for me that I might develop the same kind of loving respect for this most sacred gift from Our Lord.

June 3

"Without a doubt, it's a great grace to receive the sacraments; but when God doesn't allow it, it's good just the same."

There was a time, during the coronavirus pandemic, that many Catholics around the world were unable to receive the sacraments due to public health concerns. As painful as this deprivation was, Thérèse reminds us that if God's permissive will allows such a circumstance, we must accept it. Do I accept God's permissive will when it causes me to suffer something very painful? Do I need to ask for a special grace during these times so that I might obey as willingly as Thérèse suggests?

Dear Thérèse, I need so much help in learning how to accept God's will in difficult times. Help me to admit my weakness in this area and ask God for the grace I need to be more accepting of all that He allows to happen to me, confident that His grace will give me the strength to endure even the worst of times.

June 4

*"Dying after receiving Holy Communion would be too
beautiful for me; little souls couldn't imitate this."*

❧

When Thérèse's life was nearing its end, the sisters
would often speculate as to when this event might
occur. However, Thérèse was adamant that she
didn't want anything spectacular to happen at that
moment because she wanted little souls to be able
to imitate her. Have I ever considered that being
"little" is special enough and that I don't need
anything spiritually spectacular to happen to me to
make me holier? Am I content with this?

❧

*Little Flower, help me to understand that in spite of its
ordinariness, your Little Way is truly exceptional in the eyes
of God because it helps me to be like the child whom Jesus
invites to "come unto me" (Matt: 19:14).*

June 5

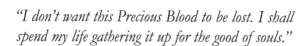

"I don't want this Precious Blood to be lost. I shall spend my life gathering it up for the good of souls."

Thérèse was deeply moved by a picture of the Precious Blood dripping from Jesus into the ground beneath the cross and made a promise to never let a drop be wasted. What souls would you like to pray for today, that they might be touched by the saving power of the Precious Blood of Jesus?

St. Thérèse, allow me to join you in your quest to gather up the Precious Blood of Jesus and use it for the good of souls by praying for their conversion by the Body, Blood, Soul, and Divinity of Jesus Christ today – and every day!

June 6

"When I am before the Tabernacle, I can say
only one thing to Our Lord:
'My God, you know that I love you.'"

Thérèse's prayer life was very simple and yet heartfelt
and full of affection. If I could say only one thing to
the Lord the next time I visit Him or receive Him in
the Eucharist, what would it be?

St. Thérèse, help me to make my life of prayer more simple,
loving, and heartfelt, that it might become an even closer and
more meaningful relationship.

June 7

"I experience a living joy not only when I discover I'm imperfect, but especially when I feel I am. All this surpasses praise, which only bores me."

Thérèse valued humility above all things because this is the virtue that most attracts God. Although we all want to be praised for our spiritual abilities, it is far safer to be reminded of our littleness because it humbles us and thus makes us cling ever tighter to God. In this humility, we should rejoice! Am I able to view my imperfections in this light? How might this change the way I feel about myself?

Little Flower, I admit that experiencing my imperfections does not fill me with a living joy. Instead, they often make me feel sad, guilty, and ashamed. Please pray for me that I might be able to overcome my pride and see myself for who I am so that turning to God for help will become a natural reaction for me.

June 8

"I forgot self, and I was careful
to seek myself in nothing."

It's not easy to forget ourselves because the human instinct for preservation naturally keeps us focused on ourselves. Thérèse had the same instincts, but her great love for God and neighbor made her willingly set herself aside as often as she could. How can I imitate her today? Who can I love and serve today without seeking a reward?

St. Thérèse, I want my love for God and neighbor to become more pure and selfless, but my self-love always seems to get in the way. Please ask God to give me the grace to put myself aside, even if just in little ways, so that I might experience a taste of the joy and freedom of truly selfless love.

June 9

"God has entrusted me with graces for myself and for many others."

Thérèse was very well aware that the gifts God gave her were meant to be shared. He has been just as generous with the rest of us. What am I doing with the graces God has given me? Am I sharing them freely? In what ways can I do this today?

Dearest Thérèse, I can only thank God that you shared your gifts with the world because your Little Way has given me so much hope that I, too, can achieve holiness, in spite of my weaknesses. Help me to follow your example and share my gifts freely with others.

June 10

"When I pray for my brother missionaries, I don't offer my sufferings. I say simply: My God, give them everything I desire for myself."

What a perfect prayer – to ask God to give someone everything you wish for yourself! Only Thérèse could have thought of it! Who should I pray this prayer for today?

Dear Thérèse, what a special day this would be for me if you would ask God on my behalf today to grant me everything you desire for yourself!

On this day in 1914, Pope Pius X signed the Decree for the Introduction of the Cause for the canonization of Thérèse, referring to her as "the greatest saint of modern times."

June 11

"I can depend on nothing, on no good works of my own in order to have confidence…We experience such great peace when we're totally poor, when we depend upon no one except God."

Only the truly weak can understand the sublime wisdom in these words because only the weak know how desperately they need God's help. We will never be able to thank Him enough for the help He readily gives us, which is the source of all of our confidence. What can I do for God today to show Him how grateful I am for all the help He's given me to get this far in my spiritual life? What additional assistance should I ask Him for that might bring me closer to the goal of my life – to achieve sanctity.

Little Flower, you have taught me to be confident in God's help. Because of this, my weaknesses no longer frighten me the way they once did, but I still have work to do. Please pray for me that I might persevere in aspiring to holiness by living your Little Way.

June 12

"I am not a warrior who fought with earthly arms but with 'the sword of the spirit' which is the word of God."

❧

Thérèse knew that in order to fight and win spiritual battles, she had to use the right weapons. How often do I reach for the Word of God when my doubts arise or my faith is attacked? Do I need to put aside more time to meditate on Scripture?

❧

St. Thérèse, what better source of wisdom and support do we have than the words of Jesus? Help me to use His words as my guide, my inspiration, and my sword!

June 13

"I'll die with my weapons in my hand."

Thérèse was no quitter. Even at the end of her life, while suffering terrible physical pain and in a deep spiritual darkness, she clung to the "sword of the spirit" and let the words of Jesus be her support. What words of Jesus are the most encouraging to me? Why?

Dear Thérèse, you had few books to read in the convent and yet you found all the nourishment you needed in Jesus' Gospels. Help me to find the same inspiration in His Words that they might become the fuel that keeps me going when I am feeling discouraged.

June 14

"When I think of all the graces God gave me, I restrain myself so as not to shed tears of gratitude continually."

Thérèse had so much to be grateful for that it's no wonder she had this reaction when she stopped to think about all the graces God had given her. Can I put some time aside today to make a list of all the graces God has given me and offer Him a prayerful gift of gratitude?

St. Thérèse, how helpful it is for little souls to ponder the many graces God has given us because this not only stokes our sense of gratitude, but our confidence as well! Help me to make this exercise a regular part of my prayer life.

On this day in 1884, Thérèse was confirmed by Bishop Hugonin, the Bishop of Bayeux.

June 15

> *"As for me, I have lights only to see my little*
> *nothingness. This does me more good than*
> *all the lights on the faith."*

Thérèse did not seek extraordinary revelations from God; she sought only what was needed to achieve the sanctity God intended for her. If this meant revelations about her nothingness, so be it. Do I seek extraordinary spiritual experiences or revelations? Am I more interested in achieving a "spiritual high" than in surrendering to whatever God wills for me in my spiritual life?

St. Thérèse, help me to desire personal sanctity more than spiritual "experiences" so that I might reach whatever state of holiness God has designed for me.

June 16

"*It's because we think of the past and the future that we become discouraged and fall into despair.*"

❦

The present moment was all that mattered to Thérèse because this is where God is – and wherever He is, there also is His grace. How much time do I spend pondering on the past or the future? Do these thoughts upset or disturb me? Can I make an act of surrender today and give God my past regrets and future fears?

❦

Dear Thérèse, help me to appreciate the presence of God within me by spending more time with Him and less time in useless worry and regret.

June 17

*"I don't want to think of anything but
the present moment."*

Because she always stayed in the present moment,
Thérèse was much more aware of the gifts God was
giving her every day - from the little things like a
sunny day and a gloriously blooming garden to the
peaceful call of the birds in early morning – all
of which she shared with the God present within
her. How many of God's gifts do I miss every day
because my attention is in the past or the future?
What can I do today to remind myself to come back
to the present moment where God is waiting to
reveal His love for me?

*St. Thérèse, please give me the courage to stay in the moment
with my God so that I might experience His loving presence
and avail myself of the graces I need to face the challenges of
my day.*

June 18

"Confidence works miracles."

❦

Like so many saints before her, Thérèse knew that the way to steal Jesus' heart is through trust – the kind of blind faith in His goodness that motivated Mary Magdalen and the Good Thief to repent of a lifetime of sin and realize the miracle of conversion. How confident am I in the loving mercy of God? What makes me doubt Him? Do I still harbor feelings of unworthiness?

❦

St. Thérèse, help me to root out any lingering tendencies to doubt the goodness of our God so that I might trust Him the way He deserves to be trusted.

June 19

"What Jesus desires is that we receive Him into our hearts."

❧

Jesus wants to be more than just our "prayer God" – He wants to have a loving relationship with each of us. Thérèse was only too willing to oblige and gave her whole heart to Him. How loving is my relationship with Jesus? Is it close and personal, or am I still a bit distant, perhaps feeling unworthy to come any closer?

❧

St. Thérèse, when I come to accept my littleness the way you did, I will no longer feel as though I have to be perfect in order to have a close and loving relationship with Jesus. Help me to realize that He loves me as I am, with all my faults included.

June 20

*"There are desires God alone can understand
or rather divine."*

When we enter into a close relationship with God, it becomes apparent that He knows us better than we know ourselves. Like Thérèse discovered, He helps us to understand ourselves and the desires that motivate us. Am I willing to see myself as He sees me? What part of me can I share with Him today that will bring us closer together?

Dear Thérèse, the fact that a God as powerful and mighty as ours is interested in having a personal relationship with me is sometimes very hard to fathom. Help me to embrace the littleness that sometimes makes me feel too unworthy to call Jesus my Friend.

June 21

"How easy it is to please Jesus. We have merely to love Him without paying attention to ourselves, without examining too intently our defects."

Once again, we see the simplicity of Theresian spirituality, the central focus on loving God rather than on ourselves and our defects. How much time do I spend chiding myself over my weaknesses and failures? Might God be better served if I make a simple act of apology or contrition and then return to loving Him as I was designed to do?

St. Thérèse, don't let me be fooled into paying so much attention to my faults that I lose sight of what pleases Him the most — the gift of my love.

June 22

"What joy it is to be able to say:
'I am sure of doing God's will.'"

❧

When we are doing God's will there is a telltale peace,
even when His will entails suffering or loss. No
matter what she was experiencing, Thérèse found her
joy in what mattered most – doing God's will. Can I
challenge myself to find joy in all that God chooses
for me today, whether that be joy or sorrow?

❧

St. Thérèse, please pray for me as I prepare to abandon myself
to whatever God wills for me today and ask Him to give me
the grace to find joy in everything He chooses for me.

June 23

"He teaches me to do all *through love, to refuse Him nothing, to be content when He gives me a chance of proving to Him that I love Him. But this is done in peace, in* abandonment. *It is Jesus who is doing all in me, and I am doing nothing."*

As Thérèse teaches, when we are little and abandoned to the God Whom we love and Who loves us, He is able to do great things in us. Can I honestly say that I refuse nothing to God, or do other motivations, doubts, or fears make me hesitate?

St. Thérèse, help me to let go of my fears, once and for all, so that I might give my whole heart to God and live with Him, from this day forward, in peace and loving abandonment to His will.

June 24

"*I am not always faithful, but I never get discouraged; I abandon myself into the arms of Jesus.*"

One of the most valuable lessons to be learned in the Little Way is not to be surprised by our weakness. Discouragement comes about as a result of thinking more highly of ourselves than what we deserve, and then feeling dejected when we let ourselves down. Am I surprised by my falls? Does this make me feel discouraged and want to give up? Has it ever occurred to me that God might have allowed this fall to show me just how little I really am, and how much I need Him?

St. Thérèse, regardless of your falls, you never hesitated to repent and run straight into the arms of God, confident of His love and His mercy. Help me to cooperate with the graces God has been giving me this year, through your intercession, to never let my littleness cause me to doubt His love and mercy.

June 25

"He does not want to take anything unless we give it to Him, and the smallest thing is precious in His divine eyes."

One of God's most awe-inspiring qualities is how respectful He is of our free will. Even though He created us, and sustains us out of the purest love, He does not demand our love in return – He wants us to give it to Him because we want to do so. This truth brought a lifetime of joy to Thérèse who showered her Love with all the affection that He desired from a creature. What can I do today to shower God with all the love that He desires from me.

St. Thérèse, let us join together this day to shower the Lord with our love – yours from the eternal realm and mine from the earthly realm!

June 26

*"Jesus is a hidden treasure, an inestimable good
which few souls can find, for it is hidden, and
the world loves what sparkles."*

❧

The pursuit of riches and honor and glory were as prevalent in Thérèse's day as they are in ours – as was the dismissal of anyone who rejoiced after finding the "pearl of great price" (Matt 13: 45-46). Do I see my faith and my relationship with Jesus as a "pearl" of inestimable price? How precious is my life of faith to me?

❧

Dear Thérèse, please pray for me that I might better appreciate the gift of my faith and my relationship with Jesus.

June 27

"Your poor maid is very unfortunately in having such a bad habit, especially in being deceitful...I will really pray for her; perhaps were I in her place, I would be still less good than she is, and perhaps, too, she would have been already a great saint if she had received one half the graces God has granted to me."

❧

This comment, written in a letter to a relative, reveals the true depth of Thérèse's humility. When confronted with the faults of another, instead of becoming self-righteous and critical, Thérèse did the exact opposite and wondered how much worse she might have behaved in the maid's place. How do I react when confronted with the faults of others? How quick am I to criticize? How might I apply Thérèse's example to situations in my own life?

❧

St. Thérèse, help me to resist being critical about others and keep my eye on my own faults.

June 28

"It is the little crosses that are our whole joy; they are more common than big ones and prepare the heart to receive the latter when this is the will of our good Master."

Just like the rest of us, Thérèse had her share of crosses in life and they ranged from very large to barely a pin-prick. How do I view the little inconveniences and annoyances in my life? Do I complain about these little crosses, or do I accept them and use them to prepare me for bigger crosses, should the Lord choose to send them?

Dear Thérèse, don't let me waste my crosses! Help me to see the everyday aches and pains of life as little "tests" that can strengthen me to be a better and more docile servant of God in the future.

June 29

"I understand very well why St. Peter fell.
Poor Peter, he was relying upon himself
instead of relying only upon God's strength."

Thérèse understood just how easy it is to get carried away with our devotion and to think that we would do *anything* for God – when in reality we're capable of doing nothing without Him. While it's good to dream about doing great things for God, we must always remember that we can only accomplish these great things with His help. What do I dream of doing for God with my life? Do I understand that I can't accomplish anything without Him?

St. Thérèse, help me to never forget Who is sustaining me in this life and making all things possible for me.

June 30

*"What God prefers and chooses for me,
that is what pleases me more."*

By relying on the Holy Spirit's gift of fortitude,
Thérèse had a courageous faith and was not afraid
to let God choose her destiny. Am I able to do the
same with my life? Do I need to ask the Holy Spirit
for an increase in this gift?

*Dear Thérèse, pray for me that my confidence in God's plan
for my life might be as bold and fearless as yours!*

REFLECTIONS

FOR

July

July 1

"*You must say to God: 'I know very well that I'll never be worthy of what I hope for, but I hold out my hand to You like a beggar, and I'm sure You will answer me fully, for You are so good!'*"

This advice is well worth taking! Thérèse always believed that we get what we hope for, not because we deserve it, but because God wants to give it and will therefore answer us in His own way and His own time. How much do I hope for from God? Do I measure my hopes on what I think I deserve? What do I think God, in His goodness, wants for me to hope?

Little Flower, you were so confident in God because you trusted wholeheartedly in His goodness. Help me to trust in His love so that I might hope for what He wants to give in spite of how little I deserve it.

July 2

"A soldier is not afraid of combat, and I am a soldier."

The word "fear" was not in Thérèse's lexicon. When she felt unsure or troubled, she turned instantly to God for the grace to put aside her fear so that she could continue to love and serve Him. How much do I let fear stand in the way of my service to God? Of what am I afraid? Is this something I need to take to prayer today?

Dearest Thérèse, help me to understand that the secret to being a brave little soul is to rely on God and not myself!

July 3

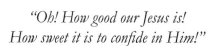

"Oh! How good our Jesus is!
How sweet it is to confide in Him!"

❦

Thérèse hid nothing from Jesus. He was truly her best friend in Whom she confided all of her secrets. Is this the kind of relationship I have with Jesus? What might be holding me back from confiding in Him? Do I feel unworthy to enjoy such a personal relationship with Jesus?

❦

St. Thérèse, I need a confidant that I can trust with my life, and who better than my Creator? Please show me how to overcome my hesitancy so that Jesus and I can become true best friends.

July 4

"No, I don't remember refusing Him anything. Even when I was very little, at the age of three, I began to refuse God nothing He was asking from me."

This might sound like a high standard but remember, Thérèse was a little soul who never relied on herself. Instead, this statement is a testimony for all that God can do in the life of a docile soul. Can I remember a time when I refused God - perhaps it was a cross, or an invitation to do some work for Him? Have I asked for His forgiveness and the grace to be more generous with Him in the future?

St. Thérèse, you never refused God anything, but you still fell from time to time, and yet you always used these occasions to be reminded of what can happen when you rely on yourself rather than God. Help me to never forget how much I need His grace – and just how high I can soar if I rely upon Him rather than me!

July 5

"You must live in heaven by anticipation, for it is said: 'Where you treasure is, there is your heart also.'"

From the earliest days of her childhood, Thérèse loved to daydream about heaven which is where she would live for all eternity with "le bon Dieu" (the good God). To reach heaven was her heart's desire, which is why God was truly her treasure. Where is my treasure? How much do I treasure the gift of eternal life that Jesus won for me on the Cross? Do I need to focus more upon these supernatural treasures – and less upon my earthbound treasures?

Dearest Thérèse, even though my upbringing was very different from yours, and we lived in two very different eras of human history, heaven is unchanging. Pray for me that I might yearn for heaven and treasure more fully the gift of eternity that Jesus won for me.

July 6

*"Let us make of our heart a little garden of delights
where Jesus may come to rest."*

❦

The images of flowers and gardens were very much a
part of Thérèse's spiritual writings. If I could design
the perfect garden for Jesus in my heart, what would
it look like? What kind of flowers (good deeds)
would be found there? What kind of fragrance (acts
of love for God) would fill the air? When do I need
to begin creating this garden in my soul?

❦

*St. Thérèse, please ask Jesus to grant me the grace to pay more
attention to beautifying my soul so that it might become for
Him a lovely, fragrant garden of love.*

July 7

"Why fear the storm when the heavens are serene?"

Even when the ever-worsening tuberculosis darkened her future, Thérèse remained in the present moment, availing herself of all the graces God had for her in that moment, certain that He would be there for her no matter what the future brought. Do I often worry about the future? What about the future worries me the most? Am I confident that I can give those worries to Jesus because He will be there for me with all the graces I need when those future storms arrive?

St. Thérèse, help me to leave my worries about future storms with God and remain focused on the here-and-now so that I won't miss a single drop of grace that God has in store for me today.

July 8

"My life hasn't been bitter, because I knew how to turn all bitterness into something joyful and sweet."

When we suffer for someone we love, the suffering is still painful, but it is somehow sweeter. Because Thérèse saw everything that happened to her as coming from the hand of God Who loved her, there was something sweet to be found in every moment of life, even the painful ones. Am I able to discern the loving hand of God in the darker events of my life? Do I even try?

St. Thérèse, pray for me that in those painful moments of life, I will be able to see the hand of God working for my good, in spite of how it might feel at the moment.

July 9

"I feel my prayer does not tire Jesus;
knowing the helplessness of His poor little spouse,
He is content with her good will."

Thérèse never considered herself to be a great mystic like the founder of her order, the great St. Teresa of Avila. In fact, her prayer was usually very dry and uneventful, but that didn't discourage her. As long as her intentions in prayer were formed by her good will, which was to commune with her Beloved God, she knew that Jesus was satisfied with her efforts. Do I sometimes feel discouraged when my prayer is dry or distracted, in spite of my best intentions? Do I understand that God cares more about *why* I'm praying, than *how*?

St. Thérèse, prayer can sometimes be arduous and lacking in consolation. Intercede for me that I will persevere out of love for God so I can prove to Him that I care more about pleasing Him than in pleasing myself.

July 10

*"I want to remain always little, very humble,
in order to resemble Jesus and to merit that
He make His abode in me."*

Jesus tells us that "Whoever loves me will keep my word…and we will come to him and make our dwelling with him" (John 14:23). Because there was nothing she wanted more than to be with Jesus, she made sure that she fulfilled these requirements. How much do I value the presence of God within me? Do I actively try to keep my soul as pure as possible so that it will be a comfortable dwelling place for God? Is there something special I can do today – perhaps a small sacrifice offered with love, a good deed for a neighbor, a good act of contrition or receive the Sacrament of Penance – that might freshen up my soul and make it more pleasant for my Divine Guest?

Dear Thérèse, pray for me that I might pay more attention to keeping my soul spotless for my Bridegroom.

July 11

"*God, who knows the rewards He is reserving for His friends, often loves to have them win His treasures by means of sacrifices.*"

❦

Thérèse understood that just because God's love for us is gratuitous doesn't mean we can take His blessings for granted. What can you do for God today just because you love Him and are grateful for all the rewards He has showered upon you in life?

❦

St. Thérèse, the number of rewards that God gives me every day are more numerous than I can count — and yet He asks nothing in return. Help me to give Him what He doesn't ask for — but so richly deserves — my undivided love and loyalty.

July 12

"Even in the midst of the trials He sends,
God is filled with tenderness."

❧

As Thérèse taught us during Lent this year, the crosses God sends us are tailor-made to fit our strengths, a gesture which is proof of the tenderness of His love. How have I felt this tenderness even in the darker moments of my life?

❧

St. Thérèse, it's easy to see how thoughtful and loving God is during the joyful moments of life, but I struggle to see His tenderness when things are going wrong. Help me to overlook the turbulence of my emotions during these times so that I might perceive the tenderness of His touch when I need it most.

July 13

"O Jesus, I want to love you for Yourself alone…"

It was only authentic love that enchanted the heart of little Thérèse, which is why she didn't want to love Jesus simply because of all that He could do for her. She wanted to love Him for Who He is. Although God wants us to bring our needs to Him, does asking for favors take up most of my daily prayer? Do I make any time in prayer just to enjoy His loving presence? Do I meditate on His beauty as seen in the world He created? What can I do today to love God just for Who He is, not just for what He can do for me?

St. Thérèse, I want to be much more selfless in my love for God, but my natural self-love and neediness makes this very difficult. Please pray for me that I might cooperate with all the graces God is giving me so that I will desire to love Him more purely.

On this day in 1927, the liturgical feast of St. Thérèse of Lisieux was extended to the whole Church.

July 14

"*O Jesus…I do not desire love that I feel,*
but only love that You feel."

❦

Even in our spiritual life, we all want to "feel" good, to feel loved and comforted by God. Although Thérèse accepted these gifts when God granted them to her, she was far more interested in making Him feel loved rather than herself. Can I take some time out of my prayer life today to make God feel loved by me, perhaps by telling Him of my love, of the ways that He brightens my life, of how much better my world is because I'm sharing it with Him?

❦

Dear Thérèse, help me to redirect my focus away from myself
and toward God so that I might offer many acts of love for
Him during the course of this day.

July 15

*"Be loveable toward all, no matter
with whom you are speaking."*

Even the most difficult people can become loveable
when we remember Jesus' words, "Whatever you did
for one of these least brothers of mine, you did for
me" (Matt 25:40). By keeping this in mind, Thérèse
was able to be kind toward everyone regardless of
whether she liked them. How do I treat people I
don't like? Am I able to see Jesus in those I encounter
in life? How might I put this into practice today?

*St. Thérèse, I want to do what Jesus commands, but there are
some people in my life that make this seem almost impossible to
accomplish. Please ask God to give me the grace to be loveable
toward all, even those who I don't consider to be my friends.*

July 16

"If sometimes I feel sadness, and fear coming to assail me, always supporting me in my weakness, Mother, you deign to bless me."

These verses are part of a poem written by St. Thérèse to honor Our Lady of Mount Carmel, whose feast day we celebrate today. How has Our Lady blessed me, through St. Thérèse, during this year of reflection on the Little Way? Have I come to appreciate the childlike love and confidence Thérèse had in Mary? How can I imitate this loving confidence in Mary today by bringing her my fears and sorrows and accepted her support and blessings?

Dearest Thérèse, give me your childlike love for Mary and help me to rely upon her as completely as you did in life.

July 17

"Be happy out of virtue, not whim."

⬥

What wisdom is hidden in this simple sentiment! Thérèse is warning us not to base our happiness upon the inconsequential and material things of life. Instead, we should find it in what matters – love for God and neighbor. What makes me happy in life? Possessions? People? Faith? Can I rank the sources of my happiness? Where is God in this ranking?

⬥

St. Thérèse, help me to find my joy in what truly matters in life and to not let my heart be seduced by the fleeting joys of sensual and material delights.

July 18

*"When you are sad, forget yourself
and show cheerfulness."*

This is much easier said than done, and Thérèse knew this. Even she struggled to "put on a happy face" when she was feeling blue, but she relied on the grace of God to conquer her self-will. How do I act around others when I am down in the dumps? Do I drag them down with me or do I put on a cheerful face?

St. Thérèse, help me to get over my need for pity and be more thoughtful of the feelings of others today.

July 19

"If every tiny flower wanted to be a rose,
spring would lose its loveliness."

⬥

This sentiment is classic Thérèse! In order for God's garden to be as beautiful as He planned, every flower He designed must be included. That means me – regardless of how lovely (or unlovely) a flower I consider myself to be!

⬥

St. Thérèse, how can I learn to love God and neighbor if I don't love myself? Help me to remember that I am a child of God and no matter what my faults and failings, this fact alone makes me worthy of respect – especially from myself!

July 20

"Let us not be justices of the peace, but angels of peace."

If we want to live Thérèse's little way, we must be willing to forego being demanding and harsh and opt to use mercy and compassion as a means of ushering peace into our world. When I am faced with someone with whom I disagree, how do I react? Am I judgmental or do I make an honest attempt to understand their point-of-view? Do I get upset or do I try to keep the conversation calm and non-accusatory?

Dear Thérèse, our divisive culture makes it so difficult to relate to those with whom we disagree. Pray for me that I might resist the temptation to label and accuse and instead look for the good in those who oppose me, regardless of how they treat me.

July 21

*"Sufferings gladly borne for others
convert more people than sermons."*

❦

Time has proven that even the fiercest competitor can be won over by a display of genuine virtue in their opponent. This is especially true when someone is observed to have suffered in order to be faithful to what they believe. Am I a good example of Christian virtue to others? Does my behavior reflect Christ and lead others toward Him, rather than away from Him?

❦

Little Flower, thank you for teaching me that even little souls like me can be capable of heroic virtue simply by learning how to rely on God rather than ourselves. Help me to put this knowledge into practice and thus lead as many souls as I can to Jesus Christ.

July 22

"When one loves, one does not calculate."

There was nothing calculating or manipulative about Thérèse's relations with her loved ones. She didn't love them in order to get something in return. Instead, she loved them because they were God's creatures who reflected His image. Is there a selfish side to my love for others? Do I love others for what they can do for me, because they're God's creation - or a little of both?

St. Thérèse, I want to learn how to love purely, but I know this is impossible for humans whose fallen condition makes us vulnerable to selfishness. Help me to accept my shortcomings in this area and to do my very best to cooperate with all the graces God is giving me to overcome my selfishness.

July 23

"A word or a smile is often enough to put fresh life in a despondent soul."

How many times have we been cheered by a smile or a friendly word from someone when we were down in the dumps? Thérèse wanted to make certain she never missed a chance to be a ray of sunshine for someone in need. How can I be a ray of sunshine for someone today?

Little Flower, you were always so thoughtful of others, so willing to put yourself aside in order to make someone smile. Help me to imitate your selfless regard for others with everyone who will cross my path today.

July 24

"Each prayer is more beautiful than the others. I cannot recite them all and not knowing which to choose, I do like children who do not know how to read. I say very simply to God what I wish to say, without composing beautiful sentences, and He always understands me."

Thérèse's prayer life was a reflection of the simplicity of her soul. Rather than rely on vocal prayers, as beautiful as they are, she preferred mental prayer, which is nothing more than a simple heart-to-heart chat with God. Do I make time for this kind of heartfelt prayer every day? Can I try to devote at least 15 minutes of my prayer time each day for a friendly chat with God?

St. Thérèse, I long to draw closer to God in prayer, but sometimes I put so much pressure on myself to say so many vocal prayers that I don't have much time left to simply chat with Him and enjoy His presence. Please pray for me that I might make more time for this kind of personal contact with God each day.

July 25

"For me, prayer is a surge of the heart; it is a simple look turned toward heaven, it is a cry of recognition and of love, embracing both trial and joy."

❦

In Thérèse's view, prayer of the heart doesn't need many words. Sometimes just a glance, a sigh, a smile, is enough to communicate to God the desires of the heart. Do I see prayer as something I have to "do" rather than something that is a part of the fabric of my life? How often during the day do I turn to God to connect with Him, plead for something, or just share whatever I'm feeling? Do I need to look for ways to make my prayer more heartfelt and personal?

❦

Little Flower, help me to turn to God in all the moments of my life, not just during my prayer time.

July 26

"All God asks of you is good will."

One of the most important requirements of the Little Way is its demand for the disposition of good will. This disposition is an orientation of the will toward God along with a purity of heart and intention that protects the soul from becoming complacent about its weaknesses, which could lead them into presumption. How often do I examine my intentions during the day? For whom am I working, loving, serving – myself or God and neighbor?

St. Thérèse, it's sometimes difficult for me to keep my eyes on God, especially when the busy-ness of life takes over. Help me to begin each day with the right intention – to love and serve God in all of my words and actions.

July 27

"My whole strength lies in prayer and sacrifice, these are my invincible arms; they can move hearts far better than words, I know it by experience."

Thérèse always wanted to be a missionary and even though she lived her entire adult life in the cloister, her profound belief in the power of prayer and sacrifice saw her proclaimed the "Patroness of Missions." How much do I truly believe in the power of prayer and sacrifice? What makes me doubt these "invincible arms?" What proof of the power of prayer have I seen in my life?

St. Thérèse, help me to be faithful to the call to pray and sacrifice regardless of whether or not I ever see the fruits of my efforts in this world.

July 28

"It is because Jesus has so incomprehensible a love for us that He wills to do nothing without us. The Creator of the universe awaits the prayer of a poor little soul to save other souls like it at the price of all His blood."

❦

Thérèse was acutely aware of her partnership with God in the salvation of souls and gladly prayed and sacrificed for the souls Jesus loved enough to die for. How aware am I of this partnership with God? Do I realize that Jesus wants me to share in His work of redemption by offering my prayers and sacrifices for the salvation of souls? What can I do today to share in this sacred work?

❦

St. Thérèse, although Jesus is in need of nothing from us, He loves us so tenderly that He wants us to be a part of everything He does. Help me to cherish this desire of His and to fulfill it by becoming a more willing partner in His work of saving souls.

July 29

*"May you trust God that you are
exactly where you are meant to be."*

God doesn't make mistakes. Especially for people of good will, whose hearts are oriented toward Him, the Lord will always care for His own, even when they stray off the path He intended them to follow. What kind of signs do I look for to determine God's will for me? Do I trust that God will help me to do what He wills, or do I depend too much on my own discernment?

Dearest Thérèse, even though I know that I must do my part to discern God's will such as obeying the Commandments and those in authority over me, don't let me forget that as long as I truly want to do His will, He will help me to do so.

On this day in 1894, St. Louis Martin died at the chateau de La Musse.

July 30

"I don't want to give in order to receive."

Notice that Thérèse didn't say "I don't give in order to receive." She said, "I don't *want* to give in order to receive." She struggled with the same inherent selfishness as the rest of us; but like St. Paul, who said, "I do not do what I want, but I do what I hate" (Rom 7:14), Thérèse renounced this egotistical tendency in herself and strove to do better. Do I care for others because I want something in return? Are there strings attached to my giving? How do I feel about this attitude of mine?

Little Flower, you weren't perfect and neither am I, but at least you despised the selfishness that prevented you from loving with the pure agape love of Jesus Christ. Pray for me that I might reject this selfishness and never stop trying, with the help of His grace, to love like Jesus.

July 31

"There is only Jesus who is; all the rest is not."

Thérèse managed to encapsulate in this simple statement the very essence of humility. Jesus is God – and we are not! How easy this is to forget in a world run by the elite who are drunk on power and are turned into the "golden calves" of our time by the media. How do I view the rich and famous? Do I envy them, or pray for them?

St. Thérèse, I live in a world that values fame and fortune above all else. Help me to see the folly of this way of thinking so that I may never forget my true place in the Kingdom of God.

REFLECTIONS

FOR

August

August 1

"Let us love Him, then, unto folly."

In Thérèse's view, one can never love God too much. This is especially true in our day when we consider how maligned He is, from using His holy name in vain to disparaging His teachings and followers. What can I do today to love my God, even unto folly, in reparation for how poorly He is treated in this world?

St. Thérèse, pray that God will give me a heart that is capable of "loving unto folly" so that I can love both Him, and my neighbor, with my whole heart.

August 2

"Our mission is to forget ourselves and to reduce ourselves to nothing."

Thérèse knew that the art of loving is not about warm feelings and happy hugs. It's about forgetting ourselves that we might live wholly for others. How willing am I to give of my time, my possessions, my comforts, in order to love more whole-heartedly?

St. Thérèse, you were so generous to everyone in your life, loving even those who annoyed and offended you. Pray for me that I might cooperate with all the grace God is offering me to follow your example.

August 3

"There is only thing to do during the night…to love
Jesus with all the strength of our heart and to save souls
for Him so that He may be loved
…Oh, make Jesus loved!"

Thérèse's definition of loving Jesus unto folly
includes loving Him even when darkness falls over
our lives and we are struggling to find His light. This
kind of love is fueled by the supernatural virtues of
faith and hope. Do I need to ask God for an increase
in these virtues today so that I might be able to love
Him more faithfully, and more confidently, when
life takes a turn for the worst?

*Dearest Thérèse, pray for me that I might rely more on the
theological virtues of faith, hope, and charity, which were infused
into my soul at my baptism, so that my love for God will be
sure and steadfast, even during times of suffering and pain.*

August 4

"May the things of earth never be able to trouble my soul, and may nothing disturb my peace."

This sentiment of Thérèse reveals how carefully she kept her priorities in life. Whatever concerned her soul and her eternal destiny came first, everything else came second. For this reason, the things of earth were unable to disrupt her peace of soul. What are my priorities in life? Am I so caught up with the things of the world that I rarely reflect upon my eternal destiny? Do I consider the impact my actions of the day might have on my journey to heaven?

St. Thérèse, you lived every day with one foot in heaven and one foot on earth. Help me to arrange my priorities so that achieving heaven becomes more important than achieving the passing pleasures of the world.

August 5

"When the human heart gives itself to God, it loses nothing of its innate tenderness; in fact, this tenderness grows when it becomes more pure and more divine."

There are many who believe that if we love God first, this means our love for family and friends is somehow depleted. Thérèse knew this was not so! In fact, when love of God rules the heart, it only makes it more loving and tender toward both God and neighbor. Do I have any reservations about giving my heart wholly to God? Is there something that holds me back? Should I take this to prayer today?

St. Thérèse, please help me to understand that loving God with all my heart can never diminish my love of family and friend, but only enhance it by making it more pure and selfless.

August 6

"Knowing the extent to which each one loved himself, [Jesus] was not able to ask of His creatures a greater love than this."

How true! We human beings have a way of loving ourselves above almost anyone or anything else, and Jesus knew it, which is why He told us to "love your neighbor as yourself" (Mark 12:31). How closely do I adhere to the standard set by Jesus? Do I truly love my neighbor as myself?

Dear Thérèse, self-love often makes me love others in way that costs me the least. Help me to repent of my selfishness so that I might love as Jesus asks.

August 7

"…Charity must not consist in feelings, but in works."

❦

Thérèse said this while describing a nun in the convent who irritated her more than anyone else. In order to overcome those feelings of antipathy, she decided to treat this nun as if she loved her best of all, and from that day forward treated her so specially the nun later marveled about how much Thérèse liked her. How do I treat people who annoy me? Do I just tolerate them? Do I go out of my way to avoid them? Or do I actively try to love them as Jesus taught?

❦

St. Thérèse, please pray for me that I might have the courage to put my love for neighbor into action by putting my personal feelings aside and treating everyone as I myself would like to be treated.

August 8

*"If you are nothing, you must not forget that Jesus is
All, so you must lose your nothingness in His infinite
All...When we see ourselves as so miserable, then
we no longer wish to consider ourselves, and
we look only on the unique Beloved!"*

As we have been learning this year, Thérèse accepted her weaknesses because she relied on our omnipotent God to provide whatever she needed to accomplish His will. Do I dwell too much on my weaknesses instead of focusing on God's power and His desire to help me? How might that change in focus impact the way I perceive the journey to sainthood? Does it make achieving holiness seem more possible?

Thérèse, help me to change my focus from myself and my inadequacies to God's infinite mercy so that I can move more confidently toward my goal of sainthood.

August 9

"Love, how well our heart is made for that!"

Thérèse rejoiced in God's promise to the prophet Ezekiel (Ez 36:26) to give us "a new heart" and take away our "stony hearts" in order to give us "hearts of flesh," thus enabling us to love as we were designed to do. Imagine what this world would be like if we all lived as we were designed by our Creator! What act of charity can I offer to God today in thanksgiving for giving me a heart designed for love?

St. Thérèse, help me to remember that my heart is of flesh, not stone, and the best way to celebrate this gift is to use it to make my world a better place for all!

August 10

*"...[W]hen I feel I am able to offer nothing
...I will give Him this nothing."*

❦

Even Thérèse had bad days - when her heart was heavy, her body was wracked with illness, or she was too distracted to pray; but her great love for God was always able to find *something* to offer Him, even if it was her *nothing*. When I'm having a bad day and can barely string together two good words in prayer, do I offer this *nothing* to God? Has it ever occurred to me that How might I follow Thérèse's example the next time I'm feeling down in the dumps?

❦

Dearest Thérèse, you have helped me to see that even when I feel as if I have nothing to offer God, I can still offer Him something — my nothing! Help me to follow your example so that I might learn how to put myself aside and offer God whatever I have out of sheer love for Him, even if it seems like nothing.

August 11

"My last means of not being defeated in combat is desertion."

This adage of St. Thérèse came about one day when she and another sister were tussling over a set of keys in the hallway and accidentally woke the Superior. When the other sister unjustly blamed her, Thérèse wanted to defend herself so badly that she decided to flee rather than risk giving in to the temptation. Were there any occasions in my life when things might have turned out better if I had just turned and walked away?

St. Thérèse, help me to understand that the more I strive to acquire virtue, the stronger I will become, even if that means running away to avoid defeat!

August 12

*"The things of this earth…what do they mean to us?
Should this be our homeland, this slime,
so unworthy of an immortal soul?"*

Although Thérèse spent the latter part of her life in the austere confines of the cloister, the family in which she was raised was considered to be well-to-do. She had a personal experience of the luxuries of life, and yet still felt these were nothing in comparison to the glories to be found in our immortal soul. Do I ever look upon my soul and the supernatural gifts with which God endows it as treasures beyond compare? Can I spend some time today turning away from the worldly to focus more on the other-worldly beauty that is my soul?

St. Thérèse, pray that God will enable me to regard the riches He has placed in my soul as a treasure far greater than any I might acquire here on earth.

August 13

"Sanctity is an interior disposition which makes us humble and little in God's arms, conscious of our weakness and trusting even to audacity in the goodness of our Father."

The practice of the Little Way of Spiritual Childhood is not just something we *do*, it's what we *are*. Thérèse's way is much more of an attitude than a pious path. What is my attitude toward God? Do I see Him as a Father from Whom I do not need to hide my littleness because I trust in in His mercy. Do I need to pray for the grace to adopt this attitude more fully?

Dear Thérèse, please pray for me that I might approach God as I am – a weak soul who has nothing to offer Him but a heart full of love and trust in His mercy.

August 14

"O my God, I really want to listen to You; I beg You to answer me when I say humbly: What is truth? Make me see things as they really are. Let nothing cause me to be deceived."

Thérèse understood that the only way to learn the truth is by entering through the "narrow gate" (Matt 7:13) rather than by following the crowd where the Evil One is waiting to trap and deceive the faithful. Do I have a tendency to follow the crowd? How firmly do I stand for the faith even when its teachings are politically incorrect?

St. Thérèse, please intercede for me before the Holy Spirit and ask Him to strengthen me with His gift of Fortitude that I might be a more courageous seeker of the Truth that sets us free.

August 15

"Humility is truth."

On this glorious feast of the Assumption, let us reflect on Thérèse's definition of truth as it relates to Our Lady whose humility enabled her to accept God's will even when it cost her the life of Her beloved Son. Thérèse knew that Truth is found in the humility of knowing that Jesus Christ is Lord and that we were created to love and serve Him. Is this how I define truth? Does this help me to better understand the immense value in developing myself in genuine humility?

Little Flower, like Mary, you were a humble soul who accepted the truth of her littleness without fear because you had great confidence in God's mercy. Pray for me that I might learn this lesson well!

August 16

"If I am humble, I am entitled, without offending the good Lord, to do small foolish things until I die."

❧

In Thérèse's eyes, doing foolish things is just part of being a little soul. As hard as we try, our littleness often makes it impossible for us to get it right even though our hearts are always in the right place. What are some of the "small foolish things" that I do while striving to love and serve God with my life?

❧

St. Thérèse, even though I'm a little soul, I sometimes pretend to be bigger than I am and this never fails to lead to a fall. Help me to accept myself as a child of God in spite of my many weaknesses and my unworthiness to belong to Him.

August 17

"Our Lord needs from us neither great deeds nor profound thoughts. Neither intelligence nor talents. He cherishes simplicity."

❦

Thérèse understood the great wisdom to be found in simplicity because it is a life based on the truth – that God is the Creator and we are His creatures. As a result, the simple soul keeps its heart fixed on Christ, an accomplishment worth far more in the eyes of God than great deeds and talents. Am I careful to keep my heart fixed on Christ in order to please Him in all that I say and do during the day? Can I make a special effort to do this today?

❦

St. Thérèse, I sometimes get so busy during the day that I lose all focus on God and end up serving mostly myself and my own needs. Help me to become a more prayerful person so that I might seek God during the day just to tell Him I love Him and want to please Him in all that I do and say.

August 18

*"The only glory which matters is
the glory which lasts forever."*

❦

Long before she knew that she had contracted the
deadly tuberculosis, Thérèse lived each day as if
were her last. This helped her to remain focused
on earning heaven rather than on the praise of her
peers. How often do I consider the shortness of life
and the futility of gathering wealth and status and
praise here on earth? Is this fact of life something I
need to focus upon more?

❦

*Little Flower, even as a child your heart longed for heaven.
Pray for me that I might develop the same desire so that
achieving eternal life in heaven with God will become more of
a daily goal for me.*

August 19

"Only God can see what is at the bottom of our hearts;
we are half-blind."

How often do we think we know ourselves, but when put to the test, are shocked by our own behavior? Thérèse was well aware of this short-sightedness and warns us to remember that when it comes to the human heart, even our own, we are "half blind!" Have I ever responded to someone or some situation in a way that surprised me? What does this say about how well I know my own heart?

St. Thérèse, help me to give my whole heart to Jesus so that He might cleanse it of its many impurities and make it "like unto thine."

On this day in 1887, Thérèse received her First Holy Communion.

August 20

"Love is fed by and develops from sacrifice. The more we deprive ourselves of natural satisfaction, the stronger and the more disinterested our love [for others] becomes."

This is so true! Consider how our friendships deepen as they progress from casual conversation to being there for one another in times of trial when real sacrifice is required – thus deepening our friendship. How have I experienced this truth in my life? Who do I love enough to suffer for? Do I love God enough to suffer for Him?

Dear Thérèse, pray that God will give me the grace not to love half-way, but to love all-the-way, with my whole heart, even when it requires sacrifice and suffering.

August 21

"How easily we become impatient. We ought to be charitable and indulgent toward all without exception."

❧

Even in the cloister, Thérèse encountered personalities that sorely tested her patience, and she challenged herself to keep her feelings to herself, even if it meant fleeing the scene! How do I deal with impatience in my everyday life? Do I at least try to contain it, or do I let others know how I'm feeling? Is this something I need to take to prayer?

❧

Dear St. Thérèse, help me to be kind to everyone, especially those who test my patience, by remembering that Jesus loves them just as they are – and so should I!

August 22

*"We should never fear the battle when
the good of our neighbor is involved."*

Sometimes we have to take an unpopular stand on important moral issues, but if it means giving good example to our neighbor, then we must do so with courage and conviction. Thérèse suggests that we focus on doing good for others rather than waste time fearing the battle. How courageous am I when it comes to upholding Church teaching? Do I take a stand based on both my beliefs and my love for neighbor?

Dear Thérèse, it's so easy to cower when the battle for souls intensifies. Help me to call upon the Lord for the grace to be courageous, firm, and charitable in the profession of my faith, especially when it concerns my neighbor's eternal life.

August 23

"Be very kind…it is both an act of charity
and an exercise of patience."

Thérèse knew that the practice of kindness is not
for the faint-of-heart because of how often we
are tempted to impatience during the course of a
normal day. With the help of God's grace, can I try
to practice kindness today, from the minute I wake
up until the moment I go to bed tonight? How often
was my resolve to be kind tested today? Do I need
to take this to prayer?

---

*St. Thérèse, walk with me in this challenge to practice kindness
throughout my day. Help me to recognize those times when my
resolve is weakened and let the Spirit teach me how to rise to
these challenges in the future.*

"We must sweeten our minds by charitable thoughts. After that, the practice of patience will become almost natural."

It's much easier to be patient with people when we focus on their good qualities rather than on what makes them so irritating to us. This was a trick Thérèse used to great advantage. Is there someone in my life who tests my patience? What are his/her good qualities? Does it make me feel less impatient toward them if I focus on these good qualities instead of why they annoy me?

Little Flower, if only I could overcome my natural repugnance for certain people! Even if I can't, I can certainly take your advice and focus on their good qualities so that I might treat them in a way that is more pleasing to God. Please be with me as I take on this challenge today!

"When Our Lord withdrew into solitude, the people followed Him and He did not send them away... Imitate Him by receiving [others] graciously."

❧

In our frantic culture filled with the harried and the time-starved, this advice from Thérèse can be a real challenge. How selfish am I with my time? Am I so busy that I am no longer able to socialize, enjoy my family, or have sufficient time for quality prayer? Might this be an indication that it's time to reprioritize my life so that I can slow down and take more time to be gracious and welcoming?

❧

Little Flower, I sometimes feel crushed beneath the burden of all that is expected of me in the course of a day. Help me to take this stress to Jesus and ask for healing, hope, and the strength to make whatever changes are necessary to enable me to be more open and receptive to the needs of others.

August 26

"Charity consists in disregarding the faults of our neighbor, not being astonished at the sight of their weakness, but in being edified by the smallest act of virtue we see them practice."

How often have we listened to gossip about a neighbor and been astonished by what we were hearing? As Thérèse teaches, why should we be surprised that our neighbor has weaknesses just like we do? Instead, look for the good they do and disregard the rest. Is there someone I need to apply this teaching to today? What virtue can I find in this person? Is it possible for me to overlook his/her faults? Is this something I need to take to Confession?

St. Thérèse, please intercede for me that I will pay less attention to the misfortunes and sins of others and more attention to all the good in them instead.

August 27

"It is better to leave each one in his own opinion than to enter into arguments."

❦

Except in matters of sin, most of the arguments we enter into with others do little more than raise our own ire. As Thérèse wisely suggests, except in matters of faith, sometimes it's better to just let someone have their own opinion rather than try to prove a point or change their mind – motives which are too often founded in pride. How tolerant am I of the opinions of others when they don't agree with my own? Is the desire to prove them wrong or convert them to my way of thinking irresistible to me? Is this an urge that might need the grace of Confession?

❦

St. Thérèse, help me to overlook my need to be right if it means sparing myself and my neighbor an argument that could result in nothing more than leaving us both with hard feelings.

August 28

"It is so much more generous to give than merely to lend."

Whenever possible, Thérèse preferred to give rather than to lend, regardless of whether or not her generosity would be appreciated. How tightly do I hold onto my possessions? Are there times when I could give away something rather than just loan it to someone? What holds me back from doing so?

Dear Thérèse, help me loosen my attachment to the things of this world so that I might imitate your generous spirit.

On this day in 1877, Thérèse's mother died.

August 29

"Sentiments of charity are not enough;
they must find expression."

It's easy to say we love someone, but it's much harder to show it. Thérèse understood this and always strove to put her love into action. While it's easy to express our love for friends and family, it's much harder to do so for the poor, the marginalized, the unpopular. How do I put my love into action for the needy and the overlooked? How do I express my love toward my enemies?

Dearest Thérèse, it's so much easier to express our love verbally rather than to put it into action. Help me to make whatever sacrifices are necessary in order to show love toward those most in need.

August 30

"One must completely forget one's own ideas and tastes, and guide souls along the particular path indicated for them by Jesus, not along one's own."

Being the mistress of formation in the convent taught Thérèse a valuable lesson about the workings of the Spirit in the interior life – not everyone is called to walk the same path. She had to be constantly reminded about how God might be working in the soul of a novice and refrain from trying to make her take the same path as she had walked. Am I respectful and accepting of the way God works in the souls of my friends and family or do I try to impose my own spiritual path on others?

St. Thérèse, ask Jesus to give me the wisdom to discern the wonders of His work in souls - both in mine and others – so that I might follow His path and not my own.

August 31

"Don't hoard anything. Give away your
spiritual goods as quickly as you earn them."

Thérèse understood that God often gives us spiritual insights not just for ourselves, but to share with others in case these perceptions might be of help in their particular walk. This is especially true when it involves ways to avoid sin and temptation. How generous am I in sharing these insights with others? Am I too concerned about my spiritual reputation to share some of my mistakes so that others might learn from them?

Dear Thérèse, help me to be as generous with others as God has been with me in my spiritual life and to share freely all that He has taught me.

REFLECTIONS
FOR
September

September 1

"Lift up your eyes and see; see how in heaven there are empty places. It is your job to fill them."

❦

The call to pray for the conversion of hearts is for everyone, not just cloistered religious. How much of my prayer is devoted to praying for the conversion of hearts? Do I only pray for my family's conversion, or do I also implore God to change the hearts of lawmakers, civil and ecclesial authorities, hardened sinners, and those I consider to be my enemy?

❦

St. Thérèse, let me never forget that Jesus is calling me to share His work of redemption on earth and to regard this call as my sacred duty.

September 2

*"I do everything for God and in this way
I can lose nothing."*

What have we to lose if everything we do is for God
rather than for ourselves? Thérèse knew that this
was the secret to maintaining peace of soul because
it is our unchecked desires, needs, and yearnings that
usually cause our interior disturbances. What desires
and needs of mine frequently lead me to becoming
upset or disgruntled if they are not satisfied? Do
these desires and needs concern necessities of life,
or luxuries? Do I need to mortify my senses in order
to gain mastery over these unchecked desires?

*Dear Thérèse, you were not afraid to deprive yourself of anyone
or anything that seemed to stand between you and God. Help
me to detach from any worldly desires so that I might live a life
of closer union with God.*

September 3

*"We who run in the way of love shouldn't be thinking of
sufferings that can take place in the future; it's a lack of
confidence, it's like meddling in the work of creation."*

The future belongs to God and, in Thérèse's
eyes, any amount of anxious forethought was an
encroachment on God's territory. Yes, we must
make reasonable plans for ourselves, but not to
the point of becoming anxious about the future
because this reveals a lack of confidence in God's
providence. Am I able to make plans for the future
and leave the outcome of those plans to God, or do
I become anxious and concerned about what may or
may not happen? What does this tell me about my
level of confidence in God?

*St. Thérèse, please ask God to give me the grace to make
my future plans and leave them in His hands, trusting that
whatever He wills is the best possible outcome for me.*

September 4

"In order to love you as You love me,
I must borrow Your own love."

Thérèse didn't just want to love Jesus, she wanted to love Him as He deserved to be loved. But because her littleness made this impossible, she prayed for Him to lend her a bit of His own love – a gesture that certainly pleased Him! Can I make this prayer my own today?

Dear Thérèse, your heart was full of love for God and inspired you to think of a thousand ways to love Him, each way more endearing than the last. Pray that God might fill my heart with so much love for Him that I, too, will love Him as tenderly and thoughtfully as you did.

September 5

*"The greatest honor God can do a soul is not to
give it much, but to ask much of it."*

Thérèse took to heart the words of Jesus who said,
"Much will be required of the person entrusted with
much" (Luke 12:48) and knew that the favor of God
often comes in the form of heavier crosses rather than
material abundance. Do I see myself as favored by
God only when things are going my way? Am I able
to see the crosses He sends me as an honor and a gift?

*St. Thérèse, how wonderful it would be if the favor of God
always came to me in the form of abundance, but I know
that this is not the path that the Master walked. Help me
to mature in my spiritual life by being more accepting of the
crosses with which He chooses to favor me.*

September 6

"Real nobility is in the soul, not in the name."

❦

The wisdom of the world sees status and reputation as signs of nobility, but the wisdom of God sees otherwise. Thérèse knew that the truly noble person is one whose soul is right with God. How do I view nobility? Is it according to the wisdom of God or the wisdom of the world? Is this viewpoint something I need to challenge?

❦

Dearest Thérèse, it's so easy to be dazzled by the fineries of life, the wealth, the fame, the power and status. Help me to see that true nobility goes much deeper and is found only in the truly righteous soul.

September 7

"Serve God. He will take care of the results."

❦

Thérèse's trust in God knew no bounds! Her focus was always on serving and loving Him, and letting Him take care of the rest. Where is my focus in life? Am I about serving God or achieving a certain result? Is it possible for me to leave these results to God, or do I need to control the outcome?

❦

Little Flower, your simplicity of soul is so admirable — and yet seems so far out of reach for me. I can get so caught up in the minutiae of my endeavors that I fail to realize that I'm not giving God any room to act. Help me to sharpen my vision so that it might become more focused on the supernatural than the natural.

September 8

"The best rule is that we should follow what love inspires us to do from moment to moment, with the sole desire of pleasing the good Lord in everything He asks of us."

This rule is at the heart of Thérèse's simplicity which is a hallmark of her Little Way. She let love for God rule her motives from moment to moment. What is at the heart of my motives in life? Is it love for my comfort, for my pleasures, or for God? What can I do today to simplify my motives and make them more for God and others than for myself?

St. Thérèse, I need a lot of grace to be able to live more for God and others than for myself. Please intercede for me that I might seek and cooperate with these graces from God.

On this day in 1890, Thérèse made her final profession in Carmel.

September 9

"I say nothing. I just love Him."

When it came to prayer, Thérèse had a very simple and uncomplicated approach. Just love Him. How much of my prayer time is spent just enjoying the presence of the God whom I love? How often do I speak to Him of my love? Can I make it a point to do so today?

Dearest Thérèse, I often try to control my prayer life and spend most of the time chattering at God. Help me to devote more time to just savoring His presence within me and enjoying the love we share.

September 10

"When the human heart gives itself to God, it loses nothing of its innate tenderness; in fact, this tenderness grows when it becomes more pure and more divine."

Many people think that the Christian concept of detachment from people and things means that we can't love our family and friends, but Thérèse knew better. Learn how to love like Jesus, without expecting anything in return, naturally cures us of the attachment to others that causes us to cling and become possessive. When we let go and love for their sake alone, our love becomes stronger and more pure. How might I apply this teaching to the loves in my life? Am I clinging and possessive of them? If they didn't return my love, would I love them any less?

St. Thérèse, there is so much more to love than warm feelings! I want to love like Jesus, with a pure, selfless, supernatural love! Please pray for me that I might learn how to love without expecting anything in return.

September 11

"Why fear in advance? Wait at least for it to happen before having any distress."

Thérèse had much to fear at the end of her life while she was facing a painful terminal illness, but she refused to give in to those fears. Instead, she placed her hope in God, that He would give her the grace she needed when she was forced to face a new onslaught of suffering. Of what do I live in fear? Suffering? Deprivation? The loss of loved ones? What do these fears reveal about my trust in God?

St. Thérèse, sometimes when I think of the future, of all that could possibly happen to me, I am filled with fear. Help me to fight these fears with a lively faith and hope in God that He will get me through whatever hardships may await me in the future, just as He has done in the past.

September 12

"We cannot all be alike; there must be different kinds of holiness to glorify the divine perfections."

Thérèse often explained this concept with the analogy of flowers. In order to mirror God's magnificence and beauty, His garden needs a variety of blooms in all of the glorious shades of nature. Which one of God's perfections would I like to glorify in my holiness? His Love? Mercy? Gentleness? What kind of flower might that be?

Little Flower, instead of comparing myself to others, I'd like to find myself in the garden of God and celebrate the "little flower" that He meant for me to be so that I can glorify His perfections in my own little way.

September 13

"Great deeds are forbidden me; I can neither preach the Gospel nor shed my blood...but what does it matter? My brothers labor in my stead while...I remain close to the throne and love You for all those who are in the strife."

Thérèse never wasted time complaining about her lot in life, or her role in the Church which she often wished could be much larger and grander. Instead, she accepted the place God assigned her and used it to prayerfully support those who were in those larger and grander roles. What do I do to support the leaders in my parish and the Church? Do I pray and sacrifice for them regularly? Do I consider that my prayers may play an important role in the success of their missions?

St. Thérèse, help me to appreciate where God has placed me in the life of His Church and to do all I can to support the fellow members of the Body of Christ.

September 14

"I am sure that self-seeking leads to no good."

For the Little Flower, a woman raised in the lap of luxury who was her father's "little queen" and the pampered baby of the family, conquering her selfish tendencies was not always easy; but she knew that living for herself was not pleasing to God and she loved Him too much to live this way. In what areas of my life am I a bit too self-seeking? In my relationships, possessions, preferences?

Dear Thérèse, how I would love to be rid of the anxiety caused by all those nagging desires and "needs" that keep me focused on myself instead of on God. Pray for me that I might cooperate with the grace God is giving me to conquer this self-seeking and lead a more selfless and Godly life.

September 15

*"It is love rather than fear which leads us to
avoid the smallest voluntary fault."*

In Thérèse's mind, it was unthinkable that we would
want to avoid sin because we're afraid of God. We
should want to do this because we love Him and
don't want to offend Him. What is my motivation
for avoiding sin? Do I fear punishment, or do I fear
hurting the One I love?

*St. Thérèse, help me to avoid sin for the right reasons - because
they offend the God Who has been so good to me.*

September 16

*"He wants me to love Him because
He has forgiven me, not much, but everything."*

❧

Thérèse knew that the reason why Mary Magdalen loved Jesus so much was because He forgave her so much. In Thérèse's case, He forgave her everything, which was more than enough reason to love Him as wholeheartedly as she could. How much has Jesus forgiven me? How does this make me feel toward Him?

❧

Dear Thérèse, Jesus has forgiven me so much, and yet my love for Him is still not as deep as I would like it to be. Please pray for me that I might allow my gratitude for His mercy enflame my heart to love Him as genuinely as you did during your life on earth.

"*If the good God Himself were not to see my good deeds (which is impossible) I would not be disturbed. I love Him so much that I would want to please Him, without His knowing that it is I who am doing it.*"

Thérèse was always thinking of God rather than herself, and wanted to do things for Him out of love, not out of a desire for a reward. Do I seek to please the Lord in my words and actions out of love for Him, or because I would like something in return? What can I offer Him today with "no stings attached?"

St. Thérèse, I want to love God as selflessly as you, but my weak human nature insinuates itself into even my best deeds, making them as much for me as for the Lord. Help me to cooperate with the grace to overcome my selfishness and enjoy the ability to love God with a pure heart.

September 18

"My life hasn't been bitter because I know how to turn all bitterness into something joyful and sweet."

Thérèse experienced many heartbreaks in life – particularly when she lost her beloved parents – and even though these events were painful, they did not leave her bitter. She saw the hand of God in these events and because of her deep faith and confidence in His loving mercy, she knew that something good could be found even in these darkest events. Have the sufferings in my life left me bitter, angry, inconsolable? Am I able to see something good in these events? Do I need to take these wounds to the Lord for healing?

Dear Thérèse, you lost your mother when you were just a toddler, and your father when you were a young woman. You described these events as being the most difficult moments of your life, yet you accepted them as God's will. Help me to keep my faith in the God who allows these sad events, always remembering His goodness and mercy, so that I might turn my bitterness into newfound joy.

September 19

*"It does not matter that you have no courage,
provided you act as if you had courage."*

❦

We all know that courage doesn't mean the absence of fear. It means not letting fear stop us. Thérèse understood this adage very well and never let the more frightful moments of life stop her from submitting to God's will regardless of how it manifested. Am I a courageous defender of the Church, or do I let my fear of ridicule or retaliation cause me to back down in fear? Would I act more courageous if I had a closer relationship with the Holy Spirit, the Giver of the gift of Fortitude?

❦

St. Thérèse, pray for me that I might not let the haze of fear rob me of the courage I was given at my Confirmation to stand tall and strong for Jesus Christ. Help me to develop this precious gift by putting it to good use!

September 20

"I feel that I'm about to enter into my rest. But I feel especially that my mission is about to begin, my mission of making God loved as I love Him, of giving my little way to souls…"

Thérèse spoke these words during the last weeks of her life when she was already looking ahead to how she might serve God and His beloved children on earth from the heights of heaven. How can I return this favor to Thérèse? What can I do today to live her little way more faithfully?

St. Thérèse, even before you left this earth, you were thinking of little souls like me and how you could help us climb the steep mountain of perfection. Help me to take your little way to heart and make it my way!

September 21

"I want to spend my heaven doing good on earth."

Only the most generous heart could make such a proclamation! Even more impressive is that Thérèse did so while on her deathbed! In what ways has she spent her heaven "doing good" for me?

St. Thérèse, you have taught me so much about how to love and serve God here on earth. Thanks to you and your guidance, my journey to heaven seems much more attainable!

September 22

"God would not have given me the desire of doing good on earth after my death if He didn't want to realize it."

As far as Thérèse was concerned, there was never any reason to doubt that whatever aspirations God put into her heart, He would help her to achieve them – even dreams about what she would do in heaven! Am I confident that any dream inspired in me by God – such as to achieve sanctity here on earth - comes with a guarantee of His help? Do I sometimes feel and act as if I'm "on my own?"

Dearest Thérèse, your great confidence in God is so encouraging! Help me to see Him as an essential Partner in my spiritual journey and let Him be my "elevator" to holiness.

September 23

"I will not fear, for God will give me strength:
He'll never abandon me."

In 1897, these were the last days of Thérèse's life, and she often made these and other similar acts of faith while struggling against the unrelenting pain in her diseased lungs and intestines. To some they may seem just words, but to Thérèse and the God she loved, they were precious acts of faith. Am I able to make acts of faith when I'm in the midst of suffering? Am I able to pray, "Jesus, I trust in You; I know you'll never leave me," when it seems as if all hope is gone? Do I need to pray to be strengthened in the virtue of faith?

St. Thérèse, your faith in God was heroic, especially at the end of your life when you were suffering such extreme physical and spiritual pain. I know that this isn't because you were such a "great" soul, but because you were just the opposite – a little soul whose only hope was in God. Help me to never forget this, especially when all hope seems to be gone.

September 24

"And I who desired martyrdom, is it possible that I should die in bed?"

Thérèse truly wanted to die heroically for God, but He had other ideas. As she lay in the sparsely furnished infirmary of the Carmel of Lisieux, and realized this would be the place where God destined her to die, she could only marvel at how her life turned out. It was different than what she imagined, but God's will trumped her own ideas. Do I give God a say in my future plans? Am I willing to let Him accomplish His dreams for me?

St. Thérèse, I know that God has a dream for me, but I too often forget this and focus only on what I want and hope for myself. Help me to turn to Him and invite Him into my dreams, so that the two of us can create the outcome of my life together.

September 25

"I cannot say that Jesus makes me walk the way of humiliations exteriorly. He is content to humble me in the depth of my soul; in the eyes of creatures, I succeed in everything...I understand that it is not for my sake but for that of others that I must walk this road which appears so dangerous."

Thérèse understood the dangers of being praised and referred to as a "saint" because of how easily this can inflate a person's ego; however, Jesus kept her ever mindful of her limitations which served to protect her from dangers to her own soul even while allowing her to teach her little way to others. Do I realize the dangers of being praised for my spiritual prowess? Do I fully understand that my spiritual growth is due only to God's generous gifts and mercy?

Dearest Thérèse, sometimes you do seem like such a "big saint" to me even though I know that deep down inside, you remained very little in the eyes of both God and yourself. Help me to never forget the Giver while I enjoy the gifts of my spiritual life.

September 26

"A soul in the state of grace need never be afraid of the devil, who is such a coward that even the gaze of a child will frighten him away."

When she was a little girl, Thérèse had a dream in which she came upon a group of devils in the garden of her home. When they saw her, they ran for cover. When she pursued them, they became even more frantic as they tried to get away from her. This dream confirmed to her just how cowardly devils are when confronted with a soul in a state of grace. How much attention do I pay to keeping my soul in a state of grace, which means attending the sacraments regularly, avoiding all mortal sin, and maintaining a daily prayer life? How can I make this a higher priority?

St. Thérèse, help me to always remember that the devil can do nothing to harm me if I remain close to God in prayer and the sacraments. Like the good Father He is, "le bon Dieu" will keep me safe!

September 27

*"Life passes so quickly that it is obviously better to have
a most splendid crown and a little suffering,
than an ordinary crown and no suffering."*

❧

Very few of us pay attention to the fact that life
is fleeting, a habit that can cause us to look at life
in a near-sighted way, thus stripping it of much of
its meaning, including that of our sufferings. By
keeping her eye on heaven, Thérèse never lost sight
of the fact that everything that happened to her
here on earth had an eternal, as well as a natural,
implication. How much consideration do I give to
the shortness of my days? Does this sometimes
make suffering seem pointless to me? How aware
am I of the benefit of suffering today in order to
gain a brighter crown in heaven?

❧

*Dear Thérèse, I need to become much more aware of my
eternal destiny so that I can live my life in a way that will help
me to achieve my goal of everlasting life with God in heaven.
Please pray for me that I might acquire the ability to meditate
on eternity through the eyes of faith rather than of fear.*

September 28

"Nothing shall affright me, neither wind nor rain; and should impenetrable clouds come, O Jesus, to conceal You from my eyes, I shall not change my place, knowing that beyond the dark clouds the sun of Your love is still shining, and that its splendor cannot be eclipsed for a single instant."

Regardless of how difficult the will of God seemed to her as she neared the end of her life, Thérèse stubbornly refused to believe that God would ever abandon her, and certainly not when she needed Him the most. When I'm faced with terrible suffering, am I tempted to doubt that God is with me? Does my faith waver when I'm faced with difficulty? Do I need to take this to prayer to ask God to strengthen my faith and especially my hope in Him?

Dearest Thérèse, when things are going well for me, it's easy to believe in God, but as soon as the dark clouds come, so do my doubts and fears. Please pray for me that I might rely upon the power of God to face the darkness with courage and an undying faith in Him.

September 29

"I sing of what I want to believe, but it is without any feeling. I would not even want to tell you the degree of blackness the night is in in my soul for fear of making you share in my temptations."

In spite of how much she cherished the thought of heaven and looked forward to returning home to God, Thérèse faced her last days in the grips of a deep, dark night of the spirit, in which her usually vibrant faith was rattled to its core. In these darkest moments, she clung to what she *wanted* to believe, even though every fiber of her being was riddled with doubt. In the end, she had nothing left but blind faith. If God were to strip me of all of my delights in prayer today, how would I respond? Would I cling to Him even without the warm feelings and believe as faith and hope teaches me, that He is still there, even when I cannot feel His presence?

Little Flower, I often flounder when my prayer turns dry and my life is upset by trials. My only comfort is the thought that God is still with me, even when I can't feel Him. Help me to cling to what I know is true, and not to give in to my doubts and fears, so that I can learn how to live – and die – with blind faith in God.

September 30

"My God, I love thee."

Love for God was the story of Thérèse's life, so it was only fitting that these should have been the last words she spoke on earth. At 7:20 p.m. on the evening of September 30, 1897, she uttered these words as her eyes fixed on a space just above her beloved statue of Our Lady of the Smile. For the time it took to recite the Creed, she seemed to be in a state of ecstasy, then fell back upon the bed and passed into eternity. This was the end of the story of a little Carmelite sister in the Carmel of Lisieux - and the beginning of the story of the greatest saint of modern times.

St. Thérèse, your holy death inspires me to adopt your little way as my own, so that I, too, can face my last moments filled with love for God.

On this day in 1898, a year after Thérèse's death, the first 2,000 copies of the Story of a Soul were printed.

REFLECTIONS

FOR

October

October 1

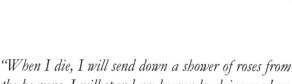

"When I die, I will send down a shower of roses from the heavens, I will spend my heaven by doing good on earth."

The feast day of the Little Flower of Lisieux is one of the most widely celebrated in the world and is the day when the "shower of roses" officially began. This little saint touched the lives of billions of people from around the world. Within just three years of her death, the Carmel of Lisieux was receiving 50 letters a day from souls around the world reporting miracles attributable to Thérèse's intercession. I want to take some time today to count my own roses from Thérèse and to give thanks to God for the gift of the Little Way.

Happy feast day, St. Thérèse! Thanks to your little way, weak souls like me can be confident that we can achieve sanctity in spite of our littleness. I pray that one day, thanks to the mercy of God, I can thank you personally – in heaven!

October 2

"If Jesus did not create you an angel in heaven, it is because He wants you to be an angel on earth."

On this feast of our Guardian Angels, we remember that Thérèse loved her angel very much and once composed a poem to him in which she referred to him as her brother, "my friend and keeper from my birth, by day and night to me most near." Can I make this the day that I increase my devotion to my guardian angel? What can I do to thank God, for the priceless gift of angelic protection and guidance? How can I be an "angel" for others today?

Dearest Thérèse, help me to develop an active spiritual relationship with my angel so that I might be more open to his inspirations and become a "messenger" of heavenly love for others.

October 3

"Discouragement itself is a form of pride. I wish, therefore, O my God, to build all my trust on you."

Thérèse understood that discouragement is very often due to our desire to have our own way, thus revealing a secret pride. How do I normally handle discouragement? Do I become irritable or give way to sulking? Could this be due to my offended pride?

Dearest Thérèse, help me to always remember to call upon God for His help in all of the events of my life so that when things don't work out as I planned, I have the peace of knowing it was God's will.

October 4

"I accept everything out of love for God."

Loving God's will for us is the secret to peace of soul because when we do this, we always get what we want! Thérèse understood this and challenged herself to accept all the ups and downs of life out of love for God and His will, which makes even the most bitter outcome sweet. How willing am I to take on this challenge today?

Dear Thérèse, pray that my love for God might overcome my love for myself so that I, too, can accept everything out of love for Him.

On this day in 1897, Thérèse is buried in the Lisieux cemetery.

October 5

"Love can accomplish all things. Things that are most impossible become easy where love is at work."

❧

True love has a power all its own. When we really love someone, there's nothing we wouldn't do for that person, no matter how difficult or even impossible it may seem. Thérèse understood this so well that she made love for God and man the guiding principle of her life – and it made her a saint! What "true loves" in my life motivate me to do great things? Does my love for God motivate me in this way?

❧

St. Thérèse, you dearly loved your family, but God was your "true love" in life and your love for Him is what motivated you to love others so purely and faithfully. Pray for me that I might grow to love Him so much that I can one day call Him my one true love.

October 6

"I assure you that the good Lord is much kinder than you can imagine. He is satisfied with a glance, with a sigh of love."

When our faith is grounded in the truth that God is all good and merciful, and that His justice is rooted in His mercy, it's easy to draw close to Him and to understand that even the smallest gesture, when offered with love, is priceless in His eyes. Thanks to her upbringing by Godly parents, Thérèse's faith in God was firmly rooted in this truth. What image of God do I have in my mind? Do I think I have to earn His love?

St. Thérèse, help me to understand God better so that I might draw closer to Him and regard Him as my God, my Friend, my Love, and my life.

October 7

"To put limits to our desires and our hopes means that we reject the infinite goodness of God."

So many people say they would be content to receive a tiny spot in heaven, but this is not the Little Way. God wants to welcome us to the highest possible spot in heaven, which is why Thérèse teaches that we must never put limits on our hopes. We must hope for all that God wants for us! What do I hope for from God? Do I hope for only what I think I deserve, or do I hope for all that God can enable me to achieve?

St. Thérèse, you based all of your hopes on what God wanted to give you rather than on what you thought you deserved. Help me to be more accepting of my littleness and how much God wants to help me achieve what I can't hope to "earn" on my own.

October 8

*"Remember that nothing is small in the eyes of God.
Do all that you do with love."*

This is the kind of teaching that gives so much hope to little souls. We may not be capable of big, bold action for God, but we can certainly love Him to the best of our ability. What little things can I do with great love for God today?

Little Flower, your teachings give me so much hope that I, too, can do great things for God, as long as my love for Him leads the way! Help me to love Him enough to let Him do great things through me.

October 9

"In little things as much as big ones, God gives even in this life a hundredfold to those who have left everything for love of Him."

Thérèse understood that God doesn't demand that we physically give up our homes or families or possessions for love of Him – just that we don't become so attached to them that they control us and rob us of our freedom. Am I too attached to my family, my possessions, my reputation? Do I let these things control me? Am I willing to let go of them for God?

St. Thérèse, your heart was like potter's clay in the hand of God, soft and pliable and easily shaped into whatever He desired. Pray for me that I might purify my heart of all inordinate attachments so that I might be formed into who God desires me to be.

October 10

"It's because we think of the past and future that we become discouraged and fall into despair."

❦

We should only look backward to learn and forward to plan but never allow ourselves to dwell on the past or future to the point of anxiety because this reveals a lack of trust in God's providence, something that is antithetical to Thérèse's Little Way. What about the past or future causes me anxiety? Is this something best left to God to resolve?

❦

Dear Thérèse, it's so hard for me to let go of the past and the future often fills me with worry. Please intercede for me before God that I might cooperate with all the graces He is giving me to remain in His presence and be more confident in His loving Providence.

October 11

"Jesus does not wish to give me provisions for the future. He feeds me from moment to moment."

Even though the Discalced Carmelites are mendicants (beggars), God has been providing for them for centuries and will continue to do so because He knows how to take care of His own. Do I go beyond what is reasonable when planning for the future? Am I able to trust in God to provide whatever might be lacking in my future resources?

Little Flower, help me to invite God into my planning for the future so that I might have the peace of knowing that my plans are in His care.

October 12

"Occasions do not make a man weak,
but they do show what He is."

What profound wisdom came from the humble lips of the Little Flower of Lisieux! In spite of her sheltered life and young age, she knew that it is the great moments of life – the successes and the failures – that reveal the truth about who we are. How did I react to the greatest successes and failure in my life? What does this reaction reveal about me? If I could do it again, how would I redo my reaction during those moments?

Little Flower, help me to focus on strengthening myself spiritually and morally so that when I am put the test in life, I wil respond with the dignity and grace of a child of God.

October 13

"Leave everything in His hands
without keeping anything in reserve."

We all know that to "let go and let God" is not as easy as it sounds, but saints like Thérèse teach us what we can achieve in life when we rise to this challenge. Am I willing to put my life, and the life of my loved ones, in God's hands? Do I give everything to God, or do I hold something back for myself because I fear giving up that much control?

St. Thérèse, I really need your help in learning how to trust God with my life — and the life of my loved ones. If I can't trust Him with these precious lives here on earth, how can I trust Him to bring us safely to our eternal home? Please intercede for me that I might cooperate with the grace to truly 'let go and let God'."

October 14

"O Jesus, obedience is the compass you have given me to lead me to the eternal shore."

We don't have to be in a religious order to appreciate the value of the virtue of obedience. As Thérèse teaches, no one can walk her Little Way unless they are willing to obey the will of God regardless of how it manifests. How obedient am I to the Commandments and the laws of the Church? Do I pick-and-choose what teachings of the Church I want to obey? How respectful am I of the legitimate authority in my life – my boss, pastor, civil authorities? Do I obey all laws with the exception of those that allow sin?

St. Thérèse, only the truly humble can understand the value of the virtue of obedience because humility strips away the veil and reveals the will of God working through those who have been given authority over me. I want to obey God's will, no matter how – or through whom – it manifests in my life.

On this day in 1997, Pope John Paul II declared Thérèse a Doctor of the Church

October 15

*"What a joy it is for me to fix my glance upon you
and then to accomplish your will."*

Regardless of how God's will manifested in her life – whether it be the death of a parent, the accomplishment of a lifelong goal, or contracting a terminal illness – Thérèse was able to keep her sight focused on God who loved her, confident that His will was sourced in His love for her. Am I able to see the hand of a loving God in my life, even when things go wrong? Do I allow my emotions to rule my faith and actions when life doesn't go my way?

St. Thérèse, please ask God to give me the grace to strengthen my will so that I can remain steadfast and focused on accomplishing His will during the best – and worst – moments of life.

October 16

"Souls on fire with love cannot remain inactive."

❦

It's impossible to love someone and yet resist the urge to proclaim the wonders of your beloved to the world. Thérèse's great love for God would never allow her to remain silent and neglect the opportunity to proclaim His glories to the world. What do I do to share the glories of God's love for me? How do I put my love for God into action every day?

❦

Dearest Thérèse, ask God to set my heart aflame for Him so that I can help you to accomplish your mission of "making Love loved" here on earth.

October 17

"I feel always the same audacious confidence that I will become a great saint, for I do not count on my own merits since I have none, but I hope in Him."

As Thérèse teaches, there is nothing prideful about the soul who aspires to sainthood out of love for God and with full recognition of our absolute need of His help in order to achieve that level of sanctity. How much do I desire to become a saint? Am I afraid of what becoming a saint might require of me?

Dear Thérèse, don't let me fall into the trap of believing sainthood is made for souls who are greater than me because these thoughts come from pride and a secret self-reliance on myself. Help me to understand that the smaller I am and the more help I need from God is the perfect combination for sainthood!

October 18

"It is only that which is eternal that is capable of satisfying our heart."

Thérèse went from living in a comfortable home to the austerities of a Carmelite cloister, a transition that taught her the value of the spiritual over the material. She gladly gave up the luxuries of life for the more profound spiritual satisfaction of living out her vocation. Where do I find satisfaction in life? When is my heart the most peaceful? Why?

St. Thérèse, even though I know that only God can satisfy my heart, I still find myself looking for satisfaction in the fleeting things of this life. Please pray for me that I might develop a supernatural vision that enables me to not only see, but to value, the riches of eternity over anything I might acquire here on earth.

October 19

"O my dear Master, I lay open my soul before You as I would expose a piece of linen to the rays of the sun."

❦

Because God is all-loving and merciful, Thérèse had no reservation about baring her soul to the Lord, regardless of what she might have done. How does the thought of baring my soul to the Lord make me feel? Are there sinful areas in my life that I would rather He didn't see?

❦

St. Thérèse, I don't want to hide anything from God, but the thought of exposing those sinful areas in my life fills me with shame and remorse. Help me to be more confident in His love and mercy so that one day I can honestly say that I hide nothing from Him.

October 20

"It is God's will that those who are still in this world should communicate heavenly gifts to one another by means of prayers."

Regardless of what she was facing in life, prayer was Thérèse's weapon of choice. How much faith do I have in the power of prayer? Do I devote as much time to praying for others as I do for myself?

St. Thérèse, help me to broaden the horizons of my prayer so that it encompasses more than just myself and my family, but this whole suffering world as well.

October 21

"Is not the apostolate of prayer, as it were, more sublime than the work of actually preaching?"

❧

This quote proves just how much faith Thérèse had in prayer. She knew that it was more powerful than preaching the faith! When I consider the grave problems facing our world today, the abortion, crime, immorality, and injustice, do I really believe that my prayer can make a difference? How much do I trust in Jesus' words that "If you ask anything of me in my name, I will do it."

❧

Dearest Thérèse, when I see the world in such turmoil, I sometimes get discouraged and think my prayers are useless. Help me to resist this temptation by understanding that God answers all of our prayers in His own time, in His own way, and according to His holy will — which may not be the way I expect!

October 22

"I just act like a child who can't read;
I tell God, quite simply, all that I want to say,
and He always understands."

❦

Thérèse didn't like complexity, especially in regard to prayer. She always went to God with exactly what was on her heart and expressed it as best as she could – then left the rest to God. How might I be overcomplicating my prayer life? Do I spend any prayer time just talking one-on-one with God?

❦

Dearest Thérèse, please pray for me that my prayer life will become less rigid and formulaic, and more heartfelt and personal.

October 23

"I have many distractions, but as soon as I am aware of them, I pray for those people the thought of whom is diverting my attention. In this way, they reap the benefit of my distractions."

Only Thérèse could turn a distraction into a blessing for someone! What do I do with my distractions in prayer? Do I allow them to frustrate me, or do I turn them into a prayer like Thérèse?

St. Thérèse, help me to understand that distractions are a part of the human condition and the worst thing to do is to allow myself to become upset over them because that only makes them worse. Please pray for me that I might rise above the annoyance of distractions at prayer and do something constructive with them — like pray for the situation or person who is distracting me!

October 24

"My nature was such that fear made me recoil; with love, not only did I advance, I actually flew..."

Thérèse grew up in a loving household which is why she naturally recoiled from the fear inspired by the prevailing notion of her day that God was a stern and punishing Being. Love was a much more motivating factor in her quest for union with God. What propels me forward in my spiritual life? Is it the desire to please the God I love, the God I fear, or a little bit of both?

Dear Thérèse, I am still in need of convincing that God is not looking for reasons to punish me for my sins, but is much more interested in forgiving and healing me. Pray that I will embrace this truth so that I, too, can fly to holiness!

October 25

"Just as the sun shines simultaneously on the tall cedars and on each little flower as though it were alone on the earth, so our Lord is occupied particularly with each soul as though there were no others like it..."

An integral part of the Little Way is the belief that God's love is all-encompassing, wide enough and broad enough and deep enough to enfold the smallest to the most glorious of souls with equal love. Do I realize that I am the "apple" of His eye (Psalm 17:8)? How does this truth make me feel about myself?

Dearest Little Flower, pray for me that I might experience the width and breadth and depth of God's love for me so that I might return that love with all the fervor of my soul.

October 26

"The affection [for the creature] is purely spiritual if the love of God grows when it grows...if by growing in one, the soul grows also in the other."

Thérèse's close family relationships taught her that when we love one another for God's sake, our love for both God and neighbor grows. Have I seen evidence of this truth in my life? Does love for my family make me love God – and them - more?

St. Thérèse, it's so important to learn how to love others for God's sake and not our own. Help me to overcome the selfishness that creeps into my relationships so that my love for others may become more selfless and enduring.

October 27

"He who walks in the love of God seeks neither his own gain nor his reward, but only to lose all things and himself for God; and this loss he judges to be his gain."

Jesus taught, "Whoever loses His life for my sake will find it" (Matthew 16:25) and Thérèse took Him seriously. When we lose everything for His sake, which we do when we learn how to love selflessly, this death to self brings about a glorious new peace because it quiets the disordered desires that torment us in life. What disordered desires are robbing me of my peace in life?

Dear Thérèse, please pray for me that I will give these troubling desires to Christ so that I can devote myself more fully to loving Him and those He desires to love through me.

October 28

*"Learn...to love God as He wills to be loved,
and forget yourself."*

Only with grace was Thérèse able to learn the vital
lesson of forgetting oneself in order to love more
selflessly. How do I think God wills me to love Him?
What action can I take today to meet this challenge?

*Thérèse, you loved Jesus with your whole being, but I fall short
of that measure. Pray for me that I may have the courage and
generosity of heart to love God as He deserves to be loved.*

October 29

"God is much better than you believe."

Thérèse never tired of speaking about the goodness of God because she wanted people to love Him as much as she did. How has my opinion of God changed during the course of my spiritual life?

St. Thérèse, please pray for me that I will not hesitate to speak about the goodness of God whenever possible so that I can convince others that He truly is much better than what we may believe!

October 30

*"I find perfection very easy to practice because
I have understood it is a matter of
'taking hold of Jesus by His Heart.'"*

As Thérèse taught, to take Jesus by His heart is to
trust Him with a confidence born from a profound
belief in His goodness and mercy. How convinced
am I of the goodness and mercy of God? Am I
convinced enough to trust Him with my life and to
follow Him wherever He wants to lead me?

*St. Thérèse, I know God is good and merciful, but I sometimes
find it hard to act on those beliefs, especially when my cross
grows heavy and my world turns dark. Pray for me that I
might train my will to trust in Him always, regardless of what
is happening in my life.*

October 31

"The smallest actions done out of love are the ones which charm His Heart."

❦

Thérèse never tired of reminding little souls that it is love, not heroic deeds, that charm the heart of God. What are the intentions behind my good deeds? Do I do them to feel good about myself, or to demonstrate my love for God and neighbor?

❦

Thérèse, help me to tear away the mask of pretension and duplicity so that I can rise to the challenge of purifying my motives.

❦

On this day in 1887, Thérèse and her father visited Bishop Hugonin at Bayeux to request permission for her to enter Carmel at the age of 15.

REFLECTIONS

FOR

November

November 1

*"I beg you to make an act of love to God and
an invocation to all the saints;
they're all my 'little' relatives up there."*

Sts. Louis and Zelie Martin lost several babies in infancy and even though Thérèse never knew these siblings, they were as much a part of her family as her living relatives. How near do I feel to those who have gone before me? Do I keep them close in prayer? Can I offer an act of thanks and love to God today for having given them to me for as long as they lived?

St. Thérèse, I want to feel the same filial closeness to the Saints in heaven that you did in life. On this feast of All Saints, please ask God to grant me the grace to appreciate the Communion of Saints and to never forget that they are as much my brothers and sisters in Christ as are my living relatives here on earth.

November 2

*"…God wills that the saints communicate grace to
each other through prayer with great love,
with a love much greater than that of a family,
and even the most perfect family on earth."*

❦

Our family of "saints" includes those in heaven, those who are suffering in Purgatory, and those who are saints-in-the-making here on earth. Thérèse kept this whole family very close in prayer and devoted herself to praying for them with great love. How much of my prayer life is devoted to praying for myself and my family, and how much is devoted to praying for those with whom I share the faith? Do I pray regularly for my brothers and sisters in Christ, asking God to keep them strong and faithful and to give them all the graces I want for myself?

❦

St. Thérèse, don't let me forget that all of the believers in Jesus Christ are meant to be united in prayer. Help me to do my part to pray for the Body of Christ so that we will all be welcomed into the Church Triumphant in heaven one day.

November 3

"With the virgins we shall be virgins; with the doctors, doctors; with the martyrs, martyrs, because all the saints are our relatives; but those who've followed the way of spiritual childhood will always retain the charms of childhood."

In Thérèse's view, all of the children of God are united in the Body of Christ whether they are part of the Church Militant here on earth or the Church Triumphant in heaven. Because of this union, we are one with the virgins, the doctors, and the martyrs; but those who followed the way of spiritual childhood and relied on God in this uniquely innocent and simple way, will maintain a special charm, even in heaven. What is it about the little way of spiritual childhood that attracts me to this path?

Dearest Thérèse, I have grown so much over this past year and have come to love my littleness like never before. Please pray that I maintain this special regard for your little way so that I too, might retain these special charms in heaven.

November 4

"How often have I thought that I may owe all the graces I've received to the prayers of a person who begged them from God for me, and whom I shall know only in heaven."

Thérèse firmly believed that everything is a grace, which is why she attributed her sanctity to God and the person He willed to pray for her, whether that be someone here on earth or in heaven. Is there a special saint who I believe prays for me and helps me in my spiritual life? Do I have a particular friend or family member whose prayers have helped me in my journey to God? What can I do today to show that person my appreciation?

Dear Thérèse, join me as I thank God today for all those who have prayed for me — my patron saint, my family members, my brothers and sisters in the faith, and those who remain a mystery to me and whose identity will be revealed only in heaven.

November 5

"In heaven we shall not meet with indifferent glances, because all the elect will discover that they owe to each other the graces that merited the crown for them."

Because of her close relationship with the Communion of Saints, Thérèse had no fear of dying and looked forward to discovering who among the elect played a part in her "crown" and whose "crown" her own prayers had helped to merit. Do I see myself as playing an active role in helping others to merit the crown of heaven? How often do I offer prayer and sacrifice for this purpose? Is it time to make this intention a daily habit?

Dear Thérèse, it makes me feel so much closer to the saints in heaven and those suffering in purgatory when I consider how closely we work together for our eternal welfare. Pray that I will be more mindful of this sacred duty in the future!

November 6

"After all, it's the same to me whether I live or die. I really don't see what I'll have after death that I don't already possess in this life. I shall see God, true; but as far as being in His presence, I am totally there here on earth."

In Thérèse's heart, there was no distance between herself and God. He was as close to her as her own breath. Can I say the same? How often during the course of a day do I stop to appreciate His presence within me?

St. Thérèse, I don't want an entire day to go by in which I neglect to acknowledge the God who resides within me by grace and who is waiting for me to notice Him, to commune with Him, to share my life with Him. Please pray that God will help me to remain forever in the state of grace so that I may enjoy His presence here on earth, and in eternity.

"It's so sweet to know one another, and to know a little about those with whom we shall live for all eternity."

Thérèse never lost sight of the supernatural reality of life. It was never just about *here* – it was always about here and *hereafter.* Have I ever considered the fact that my friends here on earth may one day also be my friends in heaven? How often do I consider the supernatural perspective of life? Am I so focused on the life I'm living here that I forget to reflect upon the eternal life that is my destiny?

Dear Thérèse, pray that I will not be short-sighted in this life and forget that I have much more than just a mortal destiny. Help me to pay more attention to my eternal destiny so that I may be prepared for that day when my Bridegroom comes to take me home.

November 8

"How unhappy I shall be in heaven if I cannot do little
favors on earth for those whom I love."

❧

These words, spoken within months of her death,
were a prelude to the shower of roses that Thérèse
would soon send to earth. What would I like to do
with my eternity? Who or what do I want to pray for?

❧

*St. Thérèse, your heart was so full of love that even after death
you wanted to continue to help others. Please pray for me that
I might develop this generosity of heart that will enable me to
aspire to loving God and others more magnanimously, both
here and in the life to come.*

November 9

"…[W]hen I gain any spiritual treasures, feeling that at this very moment there are souls in danger of being lost and falling into hell, I give them what I possess, and I have not yet found a moment when I can say: Now I'm going to work for myself."

This self-giving love was a trademark of Thérèse who believed her vocation in life was to be love in the heart of the Church. No soul was beyond the reach of her prayer and sacrifice, not even the notorious and unrepentant murderer, Henri Pranzini, whose conversion the 14-year-old Thérèse sought with the most heartfelt prayers to God. Imagine her joy when she learned that he repented just moments before he was executed for his crimes! How often do I pray for the most hardened sinners among us? Am I aware that my prayers could make the difference between heaven or hell for someone?

Dear Thérèse, you were so faith-filled and confident in God that you believed He could save even a notorious killer like Pranzini and you didn't hesitate to pray for him. Help me to be as confident in God, especially where it concerns the coldhearted sinners so prevalent in my world today whose souls are in desperate need of prayerful intercession!

November 10

"The saints of the latter days will surpass those of the first days just as the cedars surpass the other trees."

⸙

This teaching of St. Thérèse mirrors that of St. Louis Marie de Montfort who taught that the saints of the latter day would be exceptional warriors who would fight with great power and courage under the banner of Our Lady. Thérèse believed this to be true and no doubt prayed for all those who would bear this particular distinction. Do I aspire to be one of the saints of the latter days? Am I willing to let God use me in whatever way is needed to combat the evil of our day so that His righteousness and Truth will prevail? If not, what holds me back? Is this something that I need to take to prayer today?

⸙

Dearest Thérèse, when I consider the grave evils of my day, I want so badly to fight back, but fear too often stops me. Please intercede for me that I might take up the sword of the spirit and "fight the good fight" so that God's goodness and truth will one day rule our world.

November 11

"The saints encourage me."

❧

Reading the lives of the saints was something that Thérèse cherished. She was particularly fond of St. John of the Cross, the great Carmelite Doctor of the Church who wrote about union with God and how to achieve this exalted state. What saints do I look up to? Why?

❧

Dearest Thérèse, help me to find my inspiration in those saints who have gone before me. Pray that I may find all the guidance I need in the "story of their soul."

November 12

"The great saints worked for the glory of God, but I'm only a little soul; I work simply for His pleasure."

In Thérèse's eyes, the feeble efforts of devoted little souls was just as heroic in God's eyes as the works of the greatest saints. For this reason, she was content with her littleness and focused upon doing whatever she could in spite of her weaknesses – such as love God as much as she was capable. Do I sometimes strive to take on more penances, more prayer time, more fasting, than I'm capable of in the spiritual life? Do I "push against grace" and try to be bigger than I am? Am I content to do what I can, which is to love God as much as I am capable?

St. Thérèse, your little way has taught me to accept myself as I am, a small, weak, soul who can only accomplish whatever God empowers me to do. I would much rather rely on Him than myself!

"No, I don't believe I'm a great saint; I believe I'm a very little saint; but I think God has been pleased to place things in me which will do good to me and to others."

At the end of her life, Thérèse instructed her sisters to keep her nail clippings because they might one day be seen as relics of a saint. This wasn't due to her arrogance but to her utter confidence that God could make a saint even out of someone as small and weak as her, and that He would want her to share everything she learned along the Little Way. Do I think God can make me into a saint? What good might He be placing in me that I should be passing on to others?

St. Thérèse, help me to share the gifts God has given me so that my example may one day lead someone to sainthood.

November 14

"I often pray to the saints without receiving any answers; but the more deaf they are to my prayers, the more I love them."

Thérèse's confidence in the saints was founded upon her great confidence in God and the knowledge that God answers every prayer according to His will. For this reason, it hardly mattered whether she realized an answer or if it remained hidden from her. In whatever way God chose to answer her prayer, through that saint's intercession, was fine with her and had no impact on how much she loved them. Am I confident enough in God and the Communion of Saints to know He's responding to my prayers through them?

Little Flower, Scripture tells us that God cares about the birds in the sky whom He feeds without them being aware of it (Matthew 6:26). Help me to hold this truth deep in my heart, that if He cares so much for the birds, how much more must He care for me and the concerns I bring to Him in prayer?

November 15

*"What will it be then in heaven when
souls will know those who saved them?"*

❧

Thérèse loved to imagine what it would be like when she got to heaven and counted among the saints so many of the so-called infidels whom she prayed for on earth such as the murderer, Pranzini. If I died today, which one of the most "hopeless cases" that I prayed for on earth would I most like to see in heaven among the saints?

❧

St. Thérèse, your great confidence in God meant no soul was too far gone for your prayer and sacrifice. Help me to remember that my duty is to pray and let God be the judge of souls.

November 16

*"Speak to me about God, the example of the saints,
about everything that is truth."*

When the end of her life was drawing near and the
pain and anguish were increasing, Thérèse's one
delight was to hear the stories of the saints from
whom she could draw courage. How much time do
I spend reading and reflecting on the lives of the
saints? Is there some saint that I've always wanted
to learn about that I will make time to study during
this holy month dedicated to praying for souls?

*St. Thérèse, pray for me that I might find my inspiration in
the lives of holy men and women rather than in the idols of our
time, many of whom are living in ways that give bad example
to our youth.*

November 17

"And do you not think that on their side the great Saints, seeing what they owe to quite little souls, will love them with an incomparable love? … The favored companion of an Apostle or a great Doctor of the Church, will perhaps be a young shepherd lad; and a simple little child may be the intimate friend of a Patriarch.
Oh! how I long to dwell in that Kingdom of Love..."

In heaven, the playing field is always level, which is why the poor shepherd and the Patriarch can be on equal footing with the Lord – and each other. Thérèse longed to live in a world of such perfect love which can only be found in heaven. Have I ever considered that my prayers might have played a role in the making of a great saint such as St. John Paul II or St. Teresa of Calcutta? What does this truth teach me about equality in the eyes of God?

St. Thérèse, just the thought that my humble prayers and sacrifices could play a role in the making of a great saint is almost beyond my comprehension. Help me to understand that in the eyes of God, we're all equal because we have one thing in common – we were created by the same Creator who formed us out of His own perfect love.

November 18

*"Believe me, don't wait until tomorrow
to begin becoming a saint."*

❧

Thérèse was not a procrastinator, especially when it came to acquiring sainthood. The prospect of being with God in heaven forever was a powerful motivator for her. How much thought do I give to the quest for sainthood? Does the thought of going to heaven motivate me to strive for holiness?

❧

St. Thérèse, please pray for me that God will fill me with the desire to become a saint so that I can one day meet Him face-to-face and live in Him for all eternity.

November 19

"Let us not forget souls, but let us forget ourselves for souls."

Selfless love isn't meant only for the living. During this month devoted to prayer for the souls in Purgatory of whom Thérèse was particularly fond, we should open our hearts in a special way to the plight of the Poor Souls. What prayer and sacrifice can I offer today to relieve the suffering of the souls in Purgatory?

St. Thérèse, help me to be generous with my prayers for the poor souls in Purgatory. Help me to never forget how much they need our prayerful support as they undergo their final purification before going home to heaven, where they will continue to pray for me.

November 20

"One day, up above in the homeland, you will see the fruits of your work. After having smiled at Jesus in the midst of tears, you will enjoy the rays of His divine Face."

❦

Although it might seem to be a thankless job, Thérèse knew that praying for souls is never a waste of time. Even if we have no inkling of the good we've done for another while on earth, in heaven we will surely know this and our joy will be complete. For whom do you weep in prayer? Does it seem like a hopeless endeavor? Are you willing to "hope against hope" (Romans 4:18) that you will see the fruits of your work in heaven?

❦

St. Thérèse, please ask God to give me the grace to remain steadfast in prayer, especially when it seems hopeless, so that I might be strengthened in faith and hope, so that the souls for whom I pray may be led to eternal salvation.

❦

On this day in 1887, during an audience with Pope Leo XXIII, Thérèse requested permission to enter Carmel at the age of 15.

November 21

"Our joy is to speak of spiritual matters, to plunge our hearts into infinity."

As so many spiritual masters have recommended, Thérèse suggests that we forego idle talk in deference to discussions about spiritual matters that will lift our hearts to God. Do I spend too much time engaging in idle talk? Do I have friends with whom I can have holy conversation?

St. Thérèse, help me to pay more attention to my eternal life in both my prayer and interaction with others so that I can be better prepared for that happy day when I will leave this earth and join my Father in heaven.

November 22

"This is the character of Jesus. He gives as God, but He wills humility of heart."

In this quote, Thérèse refers to the story of St. Peter who was unable to catch fish until the Lord instructed him on which side of the boat to toss his net. When Peter followed these instructions and caught so many fish his net nearly tore, he was immediately humbled and cried, "Begone from me, for I am a sinful man!" (Luke 5:1-11) God can be very lavish with His gifts, but He wants us to receive them humbly and thankfully. What is the most lavish gift I ever received from God, and how did I respond to it?

Little Flower, God has been so good to me that I often overlook the many gifts which He showers upon me. Help me to never become so enamored by the gifts that I lose sight of the Giver.

November 23

"We are still not as yet in our homeland, and trial must purify us as gold in the crucible."

As Thérèse knew from experience, this life is one of suffering and trial which is necessary to purify our souls in preparation for our entrance into eternity. Do I view the sufferings and trials in my life as means of purification? Am I willing to carry whatever crosses God sends me in order to achieve this purification? Do I trust Him enough to make these choices for me, or do I still want a choice in the matter?

Dearest Thérèse, even though I know how necessary it is to suffer on this earth in order to be better prepared for the next life, the mere thought of suffering makes me tremble in fear. Please pray for me that I might rely more on the grace of God to develop a more supernatural vision that enables me to see the meaning in my suffering.

November 24

*"Lord, You fill us with joy with
all the things You do for us."*

❧

Even though death was just months away, Thérèse
was filled with joy at the thought of all the blessings
God had given her. How often do I stop to enjoy
the things God does for me during the course of
a day? How can make this joyful practice a regular
part of my day?

❧

*St. Thérèse, instead of focusing on what I don't like about my
life, help me to keep my eyes fixed on the Lord's blessings so
that I can develop a more joy-filled and thankful heart.*

November 25

*"We have only the short moment of
this life to give to God."*

It's easy to view this life as never-ending, but
Thérèse's words warn us that this is not so. Our
life is very short and at the end of our pilgrimage,
we will be judged on how much we loved God and
neighbor. Am I ready to face that judgement today?

*St. Thérèse, help me to be more mindful of the shortness of my
life so that I will live each day loving God and neighbor to the
best of my ability.*

November 26

"You will see that joy will follow trial and that later on you will be happy for having suffered."

Thérèse was a woman of hope who never doubted the goodness of her beloved *bon Dieu* Who turns every hardship into a victory for those who love Him and submit to His will. Am I able to keep this truth in mind during my sufferings, or do I lose sight of it and sink into despair? Can I make a resolution to call upon Thérèse during these times to help me remember that God will turn my sorrow into joy if I surrender to His will?

Dearest Thérèse, remind me of your desire to send me a shower of roses when my skies turn dark so that I will be encouraged to accept God's will and allow Him to turn my tears into dancing.

November 27

*"This thought of the brevity of life gives me courage,
it helps me bear with the weariness of the road."*

❧

Even though she loved life, Thérèse loved the thought of being with God in heaven even more and found comfort in the reality of the shortness of life. How accepting am I of the shortness of life? Does this thought give me courage during hard times? How often do I meditate on the Four Last Things – death, judgement, heaven, and hell? Is this something I ought to do more often?

❧

Dear Thérèse, help me to find my courage in the eternal truths of my faith so that I can regard the shortness of life as a blessing and not something to fear.

November 28

"O my God, you have surpassed all my expectations."

Imagine that joy we would feel if we could utter these words to God at the end our lives! In spite of how terribly she suffered while dying, Thérèse saw only the good things God had done for her. In what ways has God surpassed my expectations? What can I do today to acknowledge this and thank Him?

Dear Thérèse, so many times God has answered my prayers in ways that went beyond what I asked or even expected. Pray for me that I will never forget how good God has been to me!

November 29

"How I thirst for Heaven - that blessed habitation where our love for Jesus will have no limit!"

❦

Notice how Thérèse thirsts for heaven, not because of what she'll get there, but for what she can give – more love to Jesus. On a scale of one to ten, with one being very little and 10 being very much, how much do I thirst for heaven?

❦

Dearest Thérèse, I want to thirst for heaven as much as you did, but I'm too often distracted by the things of earth. Please ask God to give me the grace to love Him so much that I can't wait to be with Him in heaven.

November 30

"You cannot be half a Saint. You must be a whole Saint or no Saint at all."

Thérèse was an all-or-nothing kind of person. Once she set her sight on the goal of sainthood, she was all-in. For this reason, there is no place in the Little Way for those who procrastinate or, worse, those who ask God for just a tiny inch of heaven. Thérèse asked for it all – the highest realms of heaven – not because she thought she deserved it, but because this is what God wanted for her and she never wanted to disappoint Him. Are my aspirations for sainthood lukewarm? What kind of saint do I think God wants me to be? Do I sometimes limit my expectations because I base them on what I think I deserve rather than what I think He wants to give me? Is it time for me to stop cheating myself - and God?

St. Thérèse, just like you, I want to be a whole saint, but I sometimes feel as though asking for this is prideful or even arrogant. Help me to find the courage to ask God to make me desire the sainthood He has in store for me so that I can reach whatever heights of heaven He has destined for me.

REFLECTIONS
FOR
December

December 1

"Let us remain far away from all that is vainglorious. Let us love our littleness, our lack of sensitivity. We shall then be poor in spirit and Jesus will come for us... and will set us afire with His love."

❦

There is no place for conceit or arrogance in the Little Way! Thérèse's way is not just about humility and littleness - it is about *loving* this humility and littleness – which is a far cry from anything vainglorious! How has the sense of my littleness grown in the past year, and how has this impacted my vanity? Have I noticed a new and humbler attitude growing within me?

❦

St. Thérèse, there was a time when I was embarrassed and even ashamed about my littleness, but your Little Way has taught me to accept my weaknesses and to love my merciful God who responds by drawing closer to my little soul. Pray for me that I may continue to grow in acceptance of my limitations – and in trust in God's willingness to help me.

December 2

"I long to become Love's prey."

❦

Thérèse wasn't satisfied with just loving God – she wanted to be conquered by Him, to be possessed by Him, to become totally His. How much am I willing to let myself be loved by God? Am I willing to let myself be totally His? What holds me back from giving myself more completely to God?

❦

Dearest Thérèse, please pray for me that I might finally put aside the last of my misgivings and make a total gift of myself to the Infant Jesus at Christmas this year.

December 3

"Jesus loves a cheerful heart. He loves persons who are always smiling."

❦

Thérèse's habit of smiling in spite of her feelings is one of the reasons why the sister who annoyed her the most thought she was Thérèse's best friend! Do I keep a cheerful attitude toward all, even those people whom I find disagreeable?

❦

Dear Thérèse, please remind me often today to put a smile on my face for love of Jesus — and my neighbor!

December 4

"Time is but a shadow, a dream; already God sees us in glory and takes joy in our eternal beatitude. How this thought helps my soul!"

❦

Thérèse understood that because God resides beyond the confines of time, He can already see us with Him in our eternal destiny. For those who love Him and actively seek heaven, there is nothing but joy in imagining His satisfaction in seeing us safely home. As we ponder the end times during this Advent season, how prepared am I for the appearance of my Bridegroom? Do I long for Him to come and take me with Him to heaven?

❦

Dearest Thérèse, please ask God to give me the grace to truly desire to be with Him for all eternity.

December 5

"For a long time now I have not belonged to myself;
I have given myself entirely to Jesus.
He is free to do with me whatever He likes."

Thérèse once likened herself to a little ball with which she invited the Child Jesus to play with and then throw away when He was finished with it. As I ponder the coming of the Redeemer, am I able to make the same total gift of myself to Him? Can He do with me whatever He likes?

St. Thérèse, pray for me that I might give myself to the Baby Jesus without reserve and to make a permanent place for Him within my heart.

December 6

"Ah! What peace floods the soul when she rises above natural feelings!"

Thérèse knew how easy it was to be swept away by natural feelings, which are a good and holy gift from God, but when they are not guided by faith and reason, can very often be the cause of disturbance and anxiety. This is one of the chief reasons why Christians regularly practice mortification. Do I let my emotions run unchecked, or do I strengthen my will through the practice of the virtues so that I can keep them under control and remain in the peace of Christ?

St. Thérèse, please pray for me that I will be able to focus on what this season is all about — the descent of Love to earth to redeem mankind — and not let the anxieties and pressures of holiday preparations rob me of my peace of soul.

December 7

*"It's true, I suffer a great deal—but do I suffer well?
That is the question."*

❦

Thérèse never wanted to short-change the Lord and wanted to do her very best for Him, even in suffering. What do I think it means to suffer well? Do I think it means to act heroically, to suffer without complaint, to remember to offer it up, or to be more willing to accept it? Do I realize that being a little soul like Thérèse, the only way I will ever suffer well is with the help of God?

❦

St. Thérèse, teach me to accept the fact that the only way little souls like us can suffer well is to do so with the grace of God.

December 8

"… [J]ust as in nature all the seasons are arranged in such a way as to make the humblest daisy bloom on a set day, in the same way everything works out for the good of each soul."

Thérèse was blessed with the ability to see God's hand in everything; and because she knew this hand was all-loving, no matter what He chose for her, it would be for her good. What good has come from some of the darker moments of my life? Can I see the hand of God at work?

St. Thérèse, please intercede for me before God and ask Him to give me the grace to be able to see His loving hand in all of the events of my life, both the bitter and the sweet.

December 9

"…[I]f you found a soul weaker, lowlier than mine, it would please you to fill it with still greater favors provided it abandoned itself with complete confidence to your infinite mercy."

In the eyes of the Little Flower, to be weak and lowly and yet confident in God's mercy is the perfect combination and one that can lead even the smallest soul to sainthood. After this year-long meditation on the Little Way, how much more clearly am I able to understand this truth?

St. Thérèse, I have discovered that the secret to your Little Way is confidence and trust in the mercy of God. Pray for me that my faith in Him will increase so that I can be at peace in my littleness.

December 10

"I am not disturbed in seeing myself as weakness itself. On the contrary, it is in my weakness that I glory, and I expect each day to discover new imperfections in myself."

⬥

One of the great benefits of a daily examination of conscience is that it reminds us of our weaknesses which keeps us humble. For this reason, in Thérèse's eyes, discovering our weaknesses can only be something worth celebrating. Do I make a daily examination of conscience? How do I feel when I discover a weakness in myself?

⬥

St. Thérèse, you have taught me to love my weaknesses because they keep me humble and draw God's mercy upon me. Pray that I will put this lesson into practice by admitting my weaknesses and never being too ashamed to ask God for His help.

December 11

"What a sweet joy it is to think that God is just, i.e., that he takes into account our weakness, that he is perfectly aware of our fragile nature. What should I fear then?"

Many people obey the commandments because they fear God's punishments, but this was a foreign idea to Thérèse because she found nothing to fear in God. She understood that God's justice is tempered by His mercy and love and that His dealings with us are always completely fair and never to be feared. Has this year of immersion in the Little Way given me a deeper insight into this quality of God? How has it changed my opinion of His justice?

St. Thérèse, thanks to your Little Way, I am beginning to understand the ways of God's mercy and love. Pray for me that my confidence in His justice and mercy will grow and overcome any fear that might still be lingering in my heart.

December 12

"More than ever I understand that the smallest events of our lives are conducted by God."

When we accept the truth that we are in the hands of a loving and merciful God, it gives us a peace of soul that is beyond words. Thérèse accepted this truth with great joy and abandonment. Do I see the hand of God in all of the affairs of my life, even the smallest and most inconsequential? What does this say to me about how much God loves me?

Little Flower, you always saw God as a loving Father who cared for your every need. Help me to see His hand in my life so that I can come to a deeper understanding of just how profound is His love for me.

December 13

"I don't understand souls who fear a Friend so tender."

❧

Except for those who hate God, Thérèse could not fathom a reason why anyone would fear a God as tender as ours. She saw Him not only as God, but as a true friend. How have I felt the tenderness of God in my life? Do I see Him as a Friend, a confidant, Someone with Whom to share the ups and down of my life?

❧

St. Thérèse, please pray for me that my only fear of God will be that of offending such a good Friend.

"…[T]here is only one thing to do here on earth: to cast at Jesus the flowers of little sacrifices, to take Him by caresses; this is the way I've taken Him, and it's for this that I shall be so well received."

For Thérèse, there was only one way to communicate with Jesus – from the heart. It was love that made her want to suffer for Him; love that made her trust in Him; love that kept her faithful even during the most painful trials of her life. Because she knew we will be judged on how much we loved God and neighbor, her soul was at peace as she faced her own death. If I were to stand before God tonight, would I be as confident as Thérèse that I had loved God and neighbor to the best of my ability during my life on earth?

Dearest Thérèse, I want to take Jesus by caresses, and shower Him with little flowers of sacrifice, but I get so caught up in this world that I too often forget that this is why I've been put on earth. Please intercede for me that I might receive the grace to be more recollected during the course of the day so that I don't lose sight of the God I love.

December 15

"Jesus is pleased to show me the only road which leads to this divine furnace, and this road is the abandonment of the little child who sleeps without fear in his Father's arms..."

Thérèse knew that in order for souls to draw close to this divine furnace, it is necessary to give ourselves to Him in total abandonment, with the innocent trust of a child. After this year of immersion in the Little Way of Spiritual Childhood, how much closer am I to this total abandonment to God? Is there something still holding me back? Do I need to ask God to help me conquer this impediment with the power of His grace?

Dearest Thérèse, I want to explore the depths of God's love and sleep in His arms like a child in the arms of a loving parent. Help me to be patient with myself as I make my way toward the total abandonment I seek.

December 16

"Jesus is parched. He meets with only the ungrateful and indifferent among His disciples of the world and among His own disciples. He finds, alas! Few hearts that give themselves to Him without any reservations, that understand all the tenderness of His infinite love."

❧

Nothing hurt Thérèse more than the thought of Jesus, her great Love, being rejected, even by those who were so singularly blessed by Him. She longed to offer Him the sweet nectar of her loving sacrifices to satiate His thirst for the love of ungrateful man. What can I do for Jesus today to make up for the offenses and the rejection He receives from so many in our world? Can I offer Him loving sacrifices throughout this day to ease the pain of His unrequited love?

❧

St. Thérèse, I feel so powerless when I see how little God is loved in this world. Help me to understand that every act of reparation that I make to the Sacred Heart of Jesus on behalf of this cold world is a pleasing balm upon His wounded Heart that makes up for the many offenses He suffers every day.

December 17

*"…[C]ompliments…do not inspire vanity in me,
for there is always present in my mind
the remembrance of what I am."*

❦

Thérèse made this comment about the novices she was instructing who would sometimes praise her for her wise counsel, but she considered these to be naïve sentiments made by people who didn't understand just how simple and uneducated she really was. How do I handle compliments? Do I accept them graciously and, knowing how weak I truly am, give the credit to God?

❦

St. Thérèse, it's so tempting to bask in the compliments of others! Help me to remember who I truly am so that I will always remember to give God the credit He deserves for the talents and gifts He has given me.

December 18

"If you want to feel joy, to have an attraction for suffering, it is your consolation that you are seeking since when we love a thing the pain disappears."

❧

Thérèse understood that when one truly loves Jesus, it shouldn't matter if they feel attracted to suffering because true love has a way of making pain disappear. As we approach the holy season of Christmas and the coming of the Christ Child, who are those people in my life whom I love so much that suffering for them makes the pain disappear?

❧

St. Thérèse, thank you for teaching me that true devotion barely notices the pain of suffering because the power of love casts out all fear and trepidation.

December 19

"Close to this Heart, we learn courage and especially confidence. The hail of bullets, the noise of the cannon, what is all that when we are carried by the General?"

The last thing Jesus would ever do is abandon one of His soldiers on the battlefield! Thérèse teaches us to never forget that the General of our army is carrying us and this alone should inspire us with all the courage and confidence we need to continue the good fight! How many times has darkness fallen over me and I felt abandoned by God? Looking back on those times, do I now see just how close to me He was during this time? Can I offer a special prayer of thanks to Him today for His faithfulness to me?

Dearest Thérèse, as I prepare to welcome Jesus on Christmas Day, help me to make a gift to Him of my renewed confidence and trust in His faithfulness that will never failed me in this life.

December 20

*"He is the One who makes us desire and
who grants our desires."*

❦

Thérèse teaches even though many of our passions
are disordered, it is God who inspires us with that
deepest of all desire - to know Him, love Him, and
serve Him in this life – and it is God who grants this
desire to those who ask it of Him. When was the last
time I asked the Lord to quell my inordinate desires
and increase my yearning to know Him, love Him,
and serve Him in this life with all of my heart and
soul? Will this be the day I ask Him for this favor?

❦

*Dearest Thérèse, I want to make a new commitment to my
Savior during the waning days of this Advent season so that
I might welcome Jesus into the world on Christmas Day with
a heart full of desire to conform my life more closely to His.*

December 21

"Oh how beautiful is our religion; instead of contracting hearts (as the world believes), it raises them up and renders them capable of loving."

❦

Those who cling to the true meaning of Christmas know that the most beautiful gifts to be exchanged during this season are of a spiritual, not material, nature. Thérèse knew that our hearts were made for love and it is only in God that we learn just how deeply, how selflessly, these hearts are capable of loving. Can I take time in prayer today to ask God, Who sent His only Son into the world for love of us, to teach me what it means to love with all my heart?

❦

St. Thérèse, help me to spend time this Christmas beside Jesus' cradle where He can teach me how to love without counting the cost.

December 22

*"May you not forget the infinite possibilities
that are born of faith."*

❦

For Thérèse, it is faith in God and the existence of
the supernatural realm that expands our worldview
and allows us to overcome the narrow view of
life that is the result of materialism. As I watch
the world around me be consumed in last-minute
preparations, how is my faith helping me to handle
the Christmas rush without losing sight of the
meaning of the season?

❦

*Dear Thérèse, with Christmas just a few days away, the
pressure of those final preparations is threatening to steal my
peace. Please intercede for me that I might keep my eyes fixed
on the Christ Child so that my heart will be free of all worry
and anxiety when I greet Him on Christmas morning.*

December 23

"When I speak of imperfect souls, I don't want to speak of spiritual imperfections since the most holy souls will be perfect only in heaven; but I want to speak of a lack of judgement, good manners, touchiness in certain characters; all those things which don't make life very agreeable."

Even in the convent at Lisieux, Thérèse found herself confronted with people whom she found disagreeable. Instead of faulting them, however, she let their poor behavior teach her how *not* to behave toward others. When I encounter disagreeable people during this holiday season, can I take Thérèse's advice and let them teach me how to conduct myself in ways that will make life more agreeable for others?

St. Thérèse, I can be so short of patience with those whose manners are disagreeable to me. Help me to take your advice to look for the good in them, smile through my annoyance, and learn from them how to behave in a way that will make others feel loved.

December 24

"On that night when He made Himself subject to weakness and suffering for love of me, He made me strong and courageous, arming me with His weapons."

❦

This was the night of Thérèse's famous "Christmas miracle" when she was given the grace of new strength to overcome her scruples. What special grace will I ask Jesus for on this most holy night?

❦

Dear Thérèse, please take my prayer to the throne of God and ask Him to enable me to be open and receptive to all the graces He wishes to shower upon me on this holy night.

December 25

"Let us remain close to the crib of Jesus through prayer and suffering."

Thérèse chose the name of the Child Jesus for her religious identity because she saw in Him an example of humility taken to the extreme. Imagine! The God Who created the universe, Who is the Architect of time and the Lord of Life itself, reduced Himself to that of a tiny, helpless babe just so that He could redeem sinners. On this holiest day of the year, how can I thank Him for the gift of Redemption and the price He paid to free me from my sin?

Dearest Thérèse, let us go together to the holy crib of our Infant Savior to adore Him and thank Him for the great miracle of the Incarnation that paved the way for opening the doors of heaven to suffering mankind.

December 26

*"He transformed me in such a way that
I no longer recognized myself."*

Those of us who returned to God after a life of sin can truly say with Thérèse, "I no longer recognize myself," but even those who never strayed will be transformed as they undergo ever-deepening conversion. How has my faith in God deepened over the years? How has this process changed me as a person?

St. Thérèse, please pray for me that I will never become complacent in my faith and will always strive to give more of myself to God so that I can love Him with my whole heart and soul.

December 27

"Jesus' closed little eyes speak volumes to my soul, and since He does not caress me, I take care to please Him."

Thérèse loved to meditate on the Child Jesus, not so much to gain consolation from Him, but to offer herself to Him as a toy with which the Holy Child could amuse Himself. Her focus was always on pleasing Him, not herself. How much of my relationship with God is directed to bringing me consolation, and how much is devoted to pleasing Him alone? What steps can I take today to make pleasing God a more constant focus of my spiritual life?

St. Thérèse, my selfishness has a way of creeping into everything, even my spiritual life. Help me to be more mindful of my intentions when I come to God so that I can worship Him more for His sake than for mine.

December 28

"What does me a lot of good when I think of the Holy Family is to imagine a life that was very ordinary."

Although the era in which she lived was full of sentimentality, Thérèse had a practical streak in her that emerged in some of the most unexpected places – such as how she never liked to envision the Blessed Mother or the Holy Family as being anything other than human and ordinary. It was in this way that she could more easily relate to them. Can I take some time in prayer today to meditate on the everyday life of the Holy Family? How do I imagine them confronting the normal problems of life, the monotony of chores, the demands of work, the intimacy of quiet family time? How do these reflections help me to better relate to them?

St. Thérèse, help me to see the Holy Family in a way that enables me to set them as an example for my own family life.

December 29

*"Let us work together for the salvation of souls; we have
only the one day of this life to save them
and thus to give the Lord proofs of our love."*

❦

Thérèse saw our earthly existence as being very brief which is why she believed we must do as much as possible while we're here. What better way to spend it than in loving God and proving our love by working with Him to save souls. How has this year with Thérèse inspired me to pray more for the conversion of the world? Has this prayer intention become a daily habit?

❦

Dear Thérèse, nothing grieves the heart of God more than the loss of a soul. Help me to do all that I can to pray and offer sacrifices for the conversion of souls and to see this work as a loving labor for God.

December 30

*"I trust He will not look upon my weakness
or, rather, that He will use this weakness
even to carry out His work."*

After this year-long immersion in the Little Way, hopefully we can understand more clearly why weakness should never be seen as an impediment to sanctity. In fact, as Thérèse teaches us so well, as long as our intentions are right before God, He can use these very weaknesses to shame the strong! How has my attitude toward my weaknesses changed during this year? Am I more willing to accept myself and my limitations and to realize my potential for sanctity in spite of these weaknesses?

Dear Thérèse, thanks to you, I have made progress in accepting myself with all of my weaknesses. Pray for me that I will remain committed to doing my very best for the Lord, and to surrender what I am unable do to His loving mercy.

December 31

"In heaven I'll be always with you."

❦

With these words, Thérèse reassures us that even though we've come to the end of our year in the Little Way, she will always be near us, ready and willing to help us to become like little children in the arms of our loving Father. What can I do today to show my gratitude to God for giving me the gift of the Little Flower of Lisieux?

❦

Dearest Thérèse, even though our year together has come to an end, I am not finished learning about your Little Way and will continue to use this book to deepen my understanding of this spiritual path. I thank and praise God for what I've learned thus far and give Him the gift of my confidence that He will finish the work He has begun in me!

ABOUT THE
CATHOLIC LIFE INSTITUTE

 The Catholic Life Institute, acting under the patronage of the Immaculate Heart of Mary and Our Lady of Mount Carmel, is a lay-run apostolate devoted to infusing the world with the truth and splendor of the Catholic mystical tradition as revealed by the Carmelite saints and Doctors of the Church.

The Institute was founded by members of the Immaculate Heart of Mary Chapter of Discalced Secular Carmelites from Willow Grove, Pennsylvania to introduce Carmelite spirituality and authentic Catholic contemplation to the faithful. Our programs include courses on Teresian prayer, the interior life, the Little Way of Spiritual Childhood as taught by St. Therese of Lisieux, and spiritual warfare.

Our programs are presented by Susan Brinkmann, OCDS, an award-winning Catholic journalist who serves as the Director of Communications and New Age research for Women of Grace. She is the author of several books and is a frequent guest on EWTN. Her areas of expertise are in Carmelite prayer and spirituality, the New Age, and the occult.

The Catholic Life Institute Press is our newest addition and is used to publish our workbooks and other publications. In addition to our own books, the Institute also provides a wide collection of Church-approved Catholic books at discounted prices.

Our courses, books, retreats, and seminars are faithful to the Magisterium and completely free of New Age components.

For more information, visit our website at
www.CatholicLifeInstitute.org.

Made in the USA
Middletown, DE
23 March 2021

36078036R00229